COMPLEX COPYRIGHT

For Mom and Dad

Complex Copyright
Mapping the Information Ecosystem

DEBORAH TUSSEY
Oklahoma City University School of Law, USA

ASHGATE

Published by
Ashgate Publishing Limited
Wey Court East
Union Road
Farnham
Surrey, GU9 7PT
England

Ashgate Publishing Company
Suite 420
101 Cherry Street
Burlington
VT 05401-4405
USA

www.ashgate.com

British Library Cataloguing in Publication Data
Tussey, Deborah.
Complex copyright: mapping the information ecosystem.
1. Copyright – Interpretation and construction. 2. Copyright – Codification.
I. Title
346'.0482-dc22

Library of Congress Cataloging-in-Publication Data
Tussey, Deborah.
Complex copyright: mapping the information ecosystem / by Deborah Tussey.
p. cm.
Includes bibliographical references and index.
ISBN 978-0-7546-7784-0 (hardback: alk. paper) — ISBN 978-0-7546-9532-5 (ebook)
1. Copyright—United States. 2. Copyright—Philosophy. I. Title.
KF2994.T87 2011
346.7304'82—dc23

2011026970

ISBN: 9780754677840 (hbk)
ISBN: 9780754695355 (ebk)

MIX
Paper from responsible sources
FSC® C018575
FSC
www.fsc.org

Printed and bound in Great Britain by the MPG Books Group, UK

Contents

Acknowledgements

I am indebted to participants at a number of conferences who offered useful comments on this project during the years when I was working on the book and predecessor articles. In particular, I would like to thank Peter Yu for encouraging me to pursue the subject of complexity in the intellectual property context and for inviting me to present the topic at several conferences. Thanks as well to Ann Bartow for her support of the book project, to David Lange for his feedback on the Kastenmeier experiment, and to Mike Grynberg and the rest of the faculty and staff of OCU Law School for their comments at faculty colloquia and their support throughout the project. I owe a particular debt of gratitude to Sam Lupica, for reading and commenting on this and everything else I write, and for his friendship. Thanks also to my family for their love and encouragement and, especially, to my partner Joyce Green for helping me get through the ups and downs of this project and life generally.

Deborah Tussey
May 16, 2011

Introduction: A Hitchhiker's Guide to the Information Ecosystem

The catchphrase "the information ecosystem" has become a cultural meme describing the global electronic infrastructure through which massive quantities of digitized information continuously flow in our increasingly wired society. As we spend progressively more time connected to the electronic flow, we ourselves become actors in this ecosystem. Copyright law, which is the focus of this book, affects a substantial portion of the information ecosystem: original, creative, nonfunctional expression. It governs the production and dissemination of not only obviously expressive works—such as works of art, literature, drama, and music—but also less obviously expressive works—such as software, information databases, and maps. Much of the discussion of copyright law herein revolves around American copyright law, but copyright laws of other nations receive references where appropriate.

Means of reproducing, distributing, and using such works have existed in varied forms from the inception of the written word. The ability to disseminate all forms of information expanded exponentially with the invention of the printing press, then again with the development of modern media such as films, radio, sound recordings, and television. As digital technologies replace analog technologies, the contents of many disparate media for information transmission, from novels to newspapers, movies to magazines, are reduced to homologous electronic bits that can be transmitted instantaneously over global networks and copied with ease. This transformation has created a host of problems for intellectual property law generally and copyright law in particular. The expansion of digital media has adversely impacted the profitability of many copyright industries, cutting into sales of physical products such as sound recordings, movie disks, newspapers, and reference works.[1] Attempts to adapt copyright law to the digital environment have touched off heated disputes over issues like file sharing, digital rights management, Internet streaming, and database protection, to name only a few.

---

1 Nicholas Carr, The Shallows: What the Internet is Doing to our Brains 92–3 (2010).

To date, most of these controversies have played out within the traditional, philosophic framework pitting private property rights against the public domain. Analogies to real property portray limited choices between the private enclosure and the commons.[2] An emergent thread in the copyright debate, however, rejects the analogy of intellectual property to real property. Adopting the ecosystem as metaphor, it suggests that intellectual property systems should be viewed as parts of an "information ecosystem" comparable to the ecosystems found in the natural environment. Under this view, intellectual property law, including copyright law, might profit from the application of concepts developed in environmental law.[3] If the copyright system works like an ecosystem, the goal of copyright law should be to encourage sustainable development of creative resources in a way that provides incentives to creators, yet preserves the resources essential for new creations.

The project of this book is to push the phrase "information ecosystem" past meme and metaphor and into the realm of taxonomy. Copyright systems and environmental ecosystems do not merely resemble each other, but, in fact, are members of the same category of systems—complex adaptive systems—which are nonlinear, dynamical systems, capable of evolving over time in response to changes in their environments. A large body of interdisciplinary theory and empirical research about such systems has developed over several decades, promulgated by a number of institutes and university centers, the most prominent of which is the Santa Fe Institute. Initially growing out of chaos theory, complexity theory eventually subsumed chaos theory and related areas such as network theory. Scholars in the hard and soft sciences have sought to identify fundamental characteristics of systems as diverse as natural ecosystems, the human brain, political and cultural institutions, free market economies and stock markets, and the Internet.[4] When Tim Berners-Lee, the originator of the World Wide Web, called for a new branch of science devoted to study of the Web[5], he initiated a new field of complexity study. This book suggests that most copyrightable works are created and disseminated through networks of complex adaptive systems and

---

2 *See, e.g.*, James Boyle, *The Second Enclosure Movement and The Construction of the Public Domain,* 66 Law & Contemp. Probs. 33, at 37–40 (2003).

3 *See, e.g.,* James Boyle, *A Politics for Intellectual Property: Environmentalism for the Net*, 47 Duke L.J. 87, 108–3 (1997); Peter K. Yu, *Intellectual Property and the Information Ecosystem*, 2005 Mich. St. L. Rev. 1, 7–8 (2005).

4 For an engaging, readable account of the development of complexity science, *see* Roger Lewin, Complexity: Life at the Edge of Chaos (1992).

5 Nigel Shadbolt and Tim Berners-Lee, *Web Science Emerges*, Sci. Am. (Oct. 2008), at 76–81.

that, consequently, complexity theory provides a useful lens through which we can analyze those systems and the impact of copyright law on them.

There are a few definitional hurdles that must be surmounted with regard to the meaning of the phrase "information ecosystem" and its component word "information." The phrase, as generally used, is little more than an analogy drawn between the complex systems that comprise the natural ecology and the systems by which information is created, stored, published, distributed, and used. Technology writers sometimes restrict it to physical technology: the networks, computers, smartphones, and other hardware that enable the instantaneous, global transmission of information. Other writers, including legal scholars, more typically construe it to include not merely the technology, but also the digitized content, the producers, distributors, and consumers involved in the creation and global distribution of the content, and the legal regimes that govern those activities. This book adopts the latter approach, which emphasizes the interconnectedness and interdependency of the many component systems involved in information creation and dissemination. Copyright law comprises one subsystem within the larger information ecosystem. The complexity framework proposed herein might also prove useful as applied to the different kinds of information governed by patent, trademark, or other intellectual property laws, but those speculations are beyond the scope of this book.

The definition of "information" is itself variable with context. My aging, but treasured, Webster's Collegiate offers several variations: (1) the communication or reception of knowledge or intelligence; (2) knowledge obtained from investigation, study, or instruction, including (3) facts and data but also (4) signals or characters representing data, (5) sequences of nucleotides or digital bits that produce specific effects and (6) quantitative measures of the content of information.[6] Others have defined it as anything that lowers uncertainty or, alternatively, as the output of any process.[7] Richard Dawkins, who originated the term "meme," described the meme as a unit of cultural information.[8] For purposes of this book, "information" comprises all forms of transmissible knowledge that might either be subject to protection under copyright law or excluded from it for various policy reasons. Copyright not only protects certain works from appropriation, but also contains

---

6 Merriam Webster's Collegiate Dictionary, 10th Ed., 599 (1997). The newfangled online Webster's retains the same definitions at http://www.merriam-webster.com/dictionary/information.

7 Robert Heverly, *The Information Semi-commons*, 18 Berkeley Tech. L.J. 1127, 1149 (2003).

8 Richard Dawkins, The Selfish Gene 192 (2d ed. 1989).

doctrinal limitations that assure that some information resides in the public domain, free for use by anyone, either because it has fallen out of copyright protection or because it is a kind of information, like ideas or facts, that is specifically excluded from copyright's ambit. Copyright law enables a universe of copyright-related systems, such as copyright-based industries.

Given these broad definitions, one might ask whether a mental construct like the "information ecosystem" captures the realities of the production, distribution, and use of copyrighted works. Copyright is, after all, a human-constructed system, unlike a natural ecosystem. To take an initial, high-level pass at this question, before delving deeper into complexity principles, it may be useful to "hitchhike" along with an actual copyrighted work from inception to dissemination, mapping out the paths it takes through creation, reproduction, distribution, adaptation, and use over time. A sketchy hitchhiker's guide to copyright reality may disclose whether more extensive mapping of the correspondences between the information ecosystem and natural ecosystems is likely to be fruitful.

The phrase "hitchhiker's guide" once meant, quite literally, a travel guide for hitchhikers. Today, it is more likely to call to mind Douglas Adams's popular science fiction fantasy *The Hitchhiker's Guide to the Galaxy*. It is tempting to follow that work from the moment of inspiration while Adams lay in an Austrian field in a pleasantly drunken state, to its production as a radio show, and its subsequent adaptation into a series of books, sound recordings, television episodes, and a film. The copyright complications involved in these transmogrifications of the original work inspired Adams to explain the many inconsistencies among the different versions of the tale thus:

> This was done for complex reasons of copyright.
>
> If you wish to understand these reasons, and I would suggest to you that you do not, then you should first limber your brain up with a little gentle quantum Mechanics, work out on Relativity, try really pumping lobe iron on a Unified Field Theory and then take a short cooling rest. Now you should be ready to think about copyright law, but suddenly find that you've got some much more interesting things to think about.[9]

The copyright galaxy has, however, undergone a digital upheaval since Adams wrote those words. Copyright law has become, if anything, more complex and confusing. As the global information network has expanded, copyright law has

9 Douglas Adams, The Hitchhiker's Trilogy Omnibus Edition *x* (1983).

also come to impinge on the day-to-day activities of ordinary information users in previously unimaginable ways.

Consequently, a journey through the copyright system with a more recent multipart creation, the Harry Potter books by J.K. Rowling, will more accurately portray the current copyright universe. The description that follows involves educated guesswork based on a general knowledge of publishing processes and copyright law, since the exact contents of the copyright licensing arrangements involved are, not surprisingly, unavailable to me. It should, however, provide a reasonably useful overview of the complicated processes involved in the production, dissemination, and use of such a popular copyrighted work.

According to Rowling, the idea for the books "simply fell into [her] head" in 1990 while she was delayed for four hours on a crowded train from Manchester to London. After several years spent writing the first book of the series, *Harry Potter and the Philosopher's Stone*, she found an agent who, in 1996, succeeded in placing the book with its first publisher, Bloomsbury Publishing.[10] With that placement, the wizarding world entered into the systems by which novels are published, distributed, read, and adapted. The manuscript would have worked its way at Bloomsbury through the usual publishing processes including editing, illustration, design of the physical format and materials of the book and its jacket, typesetting, printing, binding, and preparation for shipment. A marketing campaign would have been devised. A number of legal agreements would have been negotiated, undoubtedly including contracts with the illustrator, advertising outlets, book distributors, and, most importantly, of course, the contract in which Rowling gave Bloomsbury a copyright license to publish and distribute the book in the United Kingdom. Advance copies were distributed to book reviewers.

Up to this point, the book followed paths similar to that of many other novels that lie largely within the control of the author and the publisher. But here the book began to arc out on an unexpected trajectory, based on the responses of readers to the first appearance of the book. Formal reviews were generally favorable. More importantly, word of mouth began to spread among children, parents, and general readers. Children who rarely read anything were fascinated by the imaginary world of Hogwarts. Fan clubs formed. Fan sites, blogs, podcasts, and fan fiction appeared on the Internet. Academics organized symposia. The strength of the readers' responses enabled Rowling to contract publishing rights out to different publishers in many countries. Potter mania grew with every successive book in the

---

[10] J.K. Rowling, *Biography*, J.K. Rowling Official Site, http://www.jkrowling.com/en/ (last visited May 9, 2011).

series as readers anxiously awaited each new development in the wizarding world. In other words, positive feedback from millions of readers who spontaneously organized themselves into social networks with enormous market impact tipped the books over the edge from mere success to unprecedented phenomenon. The Potter books have now sold hundreds of millions of copies, been translated into over 60 different languages (including a translation from British English to American English), and adapted into a very successful series of films.[11] They have produced spinoffs in the form of toys, video games, costumes, Bertie Bot's Every Flavor Jelly Beans, and the like, which have made the Potter trademark worth billions.[12] It is, however, copyright law, not trademark law, which originally established the rights that made Rowling the first billionaire author[13] and all things Potter such a lucrative enterprise. Copyright laws, with an assist from contract law, set the rules of the game.

National copyright laws confer on authors like Rowling a bundle of rights which, with some variations among countries, may allow authors, or their assignees, to control reproduction, distribution, adaptation, public performance, and public display of their creative works. International treaties like the Berne Convention for the Protection of Literary and Artistic Works[14] and the Agreement on Trade-Related Aspects of Intellectual Property Rights (TRIPs)[15] set minimum standards for copyright protection among member nations, allowing authors like Rowling to enforce these rights in dozens of countries. Copyright establishes the legal framework under which the copyright owner can, for the lengthy duration of the copyright, license any of her rights to others or bring lawsuits against those who infringe on one or more of the rights in the bundle. Not surprisingly given the high stakes, Rowling, her publishers, and Warner Brothers studios have already been involved in a number of legal actions around the world, defending against claims that she copied the works of others, enforcing copyrights against

---

11 Guy Dammann, *Harry Potter Breaks 400m in Sales*, The Guardian (Jun. 18, 2008), http://www.guardian.co.uk/business/2008/jun/18/harrypotter.artsandentertainment /.

12 *Harry Potter Brand Wizard*, Bloomberg Business Week, (July 21, 2005), http://www.businessweek.com/innovate/content/jul2005/di20050721_060250.htm.

13 Julie Watson and Tomas Keliner, *J.K. Rowling and the Billion-Dollar Empire*, Forbes.com (Feb. 26, 2004), http://www.forbes.com/2004/02/26/cx_jw_0226rowlingbill04.html.

14 WIPO.int, *Berne Convention for the Protection of Literary and Artistic Works*, Sept. 9, 1886 as revised and amended through Sept. 28, 1979, *available at* http://www.wipo.int/treaties/en/ip/berne/rtdocs_wo001.html (last visited May 9, 2011).

15 WTO.org, *TRIPs: Text of the Agreement*, Apr. 15, 1994, *available at* http://www.wto.org/english/tratop_e/trips_e/t_agm0_e.htm (last visited May 9, 2011).

unauthorized uses, and seeking to prevent unauthorized early distribution of books in the series.[16]

Even the brief overview of the journey a single novel takes from creation through publication and distribution, and beyond, evidences an extremely complicated process potentially involving thousands (even millions) of people interacting in intricate networks. Those networks carry not only the information contained within the pages of the book itself, but also the additional information—including marketing and pricing information, sales information, and even new works like films—engendered in response to the books. Of course, the journey taken by the Potter books is hardly typical for all copyrightable works, or even for first novels. Less successful novels may garner more limited reader response, sell far fewer copies and, ultimately, wind up in remainder bins. As publishers often point out when seeking stronger copyright protections, picking the winners and losers in the business is fraught with uncertainty. Moreover, the copyright universe comprehends many other kinds of works that may follow entirely different, if equally complicated, pathways from creation through publication, distribution, and use.

The Potter films, for example, involve hundreds of people—directors, actors, screenwriters, film editors, camera crews, costumers, to name only a few—in a collective production process whose outputs are distributed globally in a number of media to millions of consumers. The newspaper reporter who writes an article on the Harry Potter success story collects data from her sources, writes her article, and releases it into a production system that reviews, compiles, formats, prints, and distributes many articles, by many different authors, in the form of a series of compilations, which may appear in both print and electronic forms and be distributed locally or globally. The lawyers and judges drafting publication contracts and arguing or deciding the Potter lawsuits are participants in an exceedingly complicated legal system, applying copyright rules that may vary considerably with respect to different kinds of works and their authors. The decisions in the cases resolving those legal issues are collected, compiled, and published through still another, quite lucrative, system dominated by several

---

16 *See,* Scholastic, Inc. v. Stouffer, 221 F. Supp. 2d 425 (S.D.N.Y. 2002) (no infringement of Stouffer's book illustrations by Potter cover illustrations); Warner Bros Ent., Inc. v. RDR Books, 575 F.Supp.2d 513 (S.D.N.Y. 2008) (unauthorized lexicon based on the Potter novels found to be infringing); BBC News, *Rowling Seeks 'Grotter' Ban*, Mar. 13, 2003, http://news.bbc.co.uk/2/hi/entertainment/2846105.stm (Rowling and publishers sue in Dutch court to enjoin Dutch distributor of allegedly infringing Russian book); David D. Kirkpatrick, *Publisher's Efforts to Keep Story's Secrets Collide with Free Speech*, N.Y.TIMES, June 21, 2003, at B6.

multinational publishing corporations. The software that powers Potter-themed games follows yet another set of production and distribution paths.

Increasingly, informational works may take a number of different paths that depend on copyright law but may actively avoid copyright restrictions. The writers of the many Wikipedia articles about Rowling and her books, for example, contribute to a cooperatively produced online encyclopedia, which follows its own production rules set by wiki software and terms of use contracts. Wikipedia's digital, noncommercial content is issued under Creative Commons and GNU General Public licenses[17] that eschew many of the restrictions imposed by copyright law in favor of free sharing of information. Numerous authors in a variety of media now release their works under such licenses.

Wikis are also among a number of new avenues for producing and distributing copyrightable works that entirely avoid traditional bricks and mortar distribution systems in favor of direct artist to consumer transactions over the Internet. Musicians like Radiohead and Wilco have, for example, successfully released recordings online directly to consumers prior to or contemporaneously with the distribution of physical copies. Millions of photographers freely share billions of photographs on Flickr. Members of social networking sites disseminate their own copyrightable works (text, photos, and the like), and share the works of others, on sites like Facebook and YouTube. Authors increasingly self-publish over the Internet. While these efforts shortcut traditional distribution pathways, the process still involves sophisticated technologies and numerous interactions.

Obviously, the substantial chunk of the information ecosystem affected by copyright law consists of many different kinds of production systems that share information with and respond to each other, as well as to economic markets, social networks, and technologies, in innumerable ways. Established legal rules, like copyright law and contract law, govern many of the interactions, but other kinds of rules, such as social norms and business practices, are also in play. Despite these accepted rules, copyright systems are also capable of producing unexpected behavior like the feedback loop that caused the Potter phenomenon.

By way of comparison, we can take a quick overview of a natural ecosystem that figures more prominently in the next chapter: the prairie ecosystem that formerly

---

[17] The GNU (GNU is not Unix) Project was founded to develop free Unix-like operating system software accompanied by a license designed to keep the software copyright-free. GNU Operating System, *What is GNU?*, http://www.gnu.org/ (last visited May 9, 2011). Creative Commons offers a number of alternative licenses tailored to allow freer uses of copyrighted works. Creative Commons, *Share, Remix, Reuse – Legally*, http://creativecommons.org/ (last visited May 9, 2011).

dominated the plains of North America. The plains soil contains microbes essential to support thousands of species of grasses that, through photosynthesis, utilize sunlight to create organic material, remove carbon dioxide from the air and release oxygen into it, and, as they decompose, return their organic matter to the soil, in a feedback loop that produces rich, black prairie earth. The grasses both feed and depend on: pollinators like bees, butterflies, and bats; herds of bison, deer, and other grazers whose foraging and wastes stimulate growth; burrowers like prairie dogs and voles whose tunneling reinvigorates root systems. Intricate predator–prey relationships exist between the species that eat grass (rabbits, mice, prairie chickens, bison) and those who eat the grass eaters (foxes, coyotes, snakes, hawks, vultures, humans). All of these are also fundamentally dependent on weather systems that provide not only sun and rain, but also the wind that scatters grass seeds and the lightning that unpredictably sets the prairies ablaze from time to time, clearing the way for new growth and discouraging infiltration by trees and shrubs.[18]

Unlike the copyright system, the prairie is a natural system of which humans are only one part. But like the copyright system, the prairie ecosystem consists of complicated, interdependent subsystems that self-organize and evolve over time. It follows some known "rules" (such as the process of photosynthesis), but also produces unexpected behaviors, like prairie fires. Even a quick tour reveals similarities in structure and behavior between the copyright-related systems that produced the Rowling books and environmental systems like the prairie, despite the fact that copyright systems are entirely a human creation while the prairie is a natural system in which human beings are implicated. They resemble each other, in their particularity, far more closely than either resembles a fenced field or a public common. In fact, they share characteristics typical of all complex adaptive systems: intricate architecture, nonlinear behavior, emergence, and adaptiveness.

Chapter 1 explains these basic complexity concepts, illustrates them with examples from both natural and human-created systems, and shows how they might apply to copyright-related systems. The chapter concludes that copyright systems seem to exhibit the characteristics typical of all complex adaptive systems. The "information ecosystem" may not be merely a convenient analogy, but may, rather, reflect the fact that copyright systems and ecosystems are fundamentally the same kind of system. That conclusion provides the foundation for two related arguments explored in the rest of the book: first, that like any complex adaptive system, copyright systems can and should be subjected to empirical analysis and,

---

18 *See* Aimee Larrabee and John Altman, Last Stand of the Tallgrass Prairie 13–37 (2001). This book is the source for subsequent discussions of the prairie ecology.

second, that, if copyright law is to encourage creativity, which emerges from the complexity of the human brain, it must be flexible enough to accommodate chaotic elements that are essential to the creative process.

The argument for empirical study is the lengthier of the two discussions, pursued in Chapters 2 and 3. Chapter 2 reviews the debate over the proper scope of copyright law that has, for three hundred years, been conducted for the most part on abstract philosophical grounds that rely heavily on reasoning by analogy to real property. The debate has devolved to a bipolar conflict between private property and the commons that does not accurately reflect the complexity of copyright systems. Empirical research into the actual effect of copyright law on the production of copyrighted works generally, or on specific copyright systems such as book publishers or the movie and recording industries, has been fairly sparse until quite recently. The focus on mere rhetoric, rather than actual proof, leaves the door open for copyright industry lobbyists who have historically exerted tremendous influence over copyright legislation, contributing to the expansion of copyright's scope and duration over the years.

Chapter 3 summarizes some of the empirical research on copyright that has been done to date. It then outlines a new approach to understanding the copyright system: holistic systems analysis based on extensive empirical research within a framework informed by complexity theory. Both quantitative and qualitative research methodologies may prove useful. Copyright scholars can do more than merely hitchhike along on imaginary journeys with a representative work or two like the Rowling books. They should be mapping out the ecology of copyright, describing the varied paths taken by the veritable cornucopia of copyrightable information. They should identify and, where possible, quantify the inputs, outputs, and processes involved in copyright production and dissemination. They should test the theories justifying copyright law against copyright's actual impacts and reconsider copyright theory in response to copyright reality.

Chapter 4 fleshes out the argument concerning the linkages between copyright, creativity, and the chaotic elements that are central to the sustainability of complex adaptive systems. Complexity science teaches that the most robust complex systems maintain a state poised between order and disorder—rather poetically referred to as the "edge of chaos." Chaotic elements provide the flexibility essential to sustainability. The human brain is a complex adaptive system and recent research in brain sciences indicates that creativity may occur at the edge of chaos. If copyright law's mission is, as claimed, to induce the production of creative works, the law should create an environment that ensures to creators not only a measure of economic support, but also freedom to engage with their culture, and with other creators. Copyright law should not impose overly rigid restraints on creative processes that are inherently unpredictable.

Finally, Chapter 5 considers how a complexity-based framework might influence lawmakers' approach to copyright law, offering a few general cautions and some specific suggestions to free up the data needed for empirical investigations and assure that the law itself responds over time to the results of those investigations. Since copyright systems, unlike environmental ecosystems, are constructed by humans and governed by human-made laws, we may hope to exert some degree of control over them, subject always to the law of unanticipated consequences. Copyright law, itself, may constitute a complex adaptive system that must be periodically retuned to remain near the edge of chaos.

The copyright system, born and bred for print technology, faces a technological revolution in its environment. Digitization and global networks have heightened the interdependence of copyright production systems, markets, and the laws that govern them. The old broadcast model of one-to-many communication is replaced with many-to-many global connectivity. The individual creativity of one author sparks the collective creativity of thousands more. Can copyright law successfully adapt to this new environment? Or will technological and social changes push copyright law, as a conceptual system, to a tipping point beyond which it ceases to be a viable means to encourage creativity?

In *The Hitchhikers' Guide to the Galaxy*, Douglas Adams dreamed up a universe in which the Earth and all its life forms comprised an enormous computational matrix designed to identify the Ultimate Question. His fictional musings may not have been far off the mark. The controversial, but putatively nonfictional, Gaia hypothesis suggests that, in fact, the Earth is a homeostatic complex adaptive system, a giant living organism, in which life maintains conditions favorable to its own survival through self-regulation. (The competing Medea hypothesis suggests that life seems to be actively pursuing its own demise.)[19] The information ecosystem may be merely one of many complex adaptive subsystems operating within a larger global system. An understanding of complex adaptive systems, supplemented by research into real copyright-related systems, may provide drafters and scholars of copyright law with conceptual tools that facilitate the crafting of flexible copyright laws that can support a sustainable information ecosystem. To put this in systems terminology, an ideal copyright law would create a self-regulating, homeostatic system in which market demand would create a feedback loop driving the creation of culture. Douglas Adams to the contrary notwithstanding, we have few more interesting things to think about.

---

19 Jascha Hoffman, *Killer Earth*, N.Y.Times Magazine, Dec. 13, 2009, at MM49.

Chapter 1
Are Publishers Really Like Prairies? Copyright Systems as Complex Adaptive Systems

It should be evident from the preceding chapter that the universe comprised of physical copyright-related systems is extraordinarily complicated. Copyright law, as a conceptual system, often strays past mere complication into near incomprehensibility. It bears the hallmarks of several hundred years in which the discipline was a backwater familiar only to copyright specialists and the copyright industries themselves. Complicatedness is not, however, the same thing as complexity. "Complexity" refers to behavior as well as structure. A complicated system like an automobile performs in a linear, predictable manner. Its overall behavior is the sum of the behavior of its parts. Complex adaptive systems, on the other hand, exhibit properties and behaviors different from those of their underlying parts. The aggregated interactions of system components produce entirely new patterns and behaviors. Complex adaptive systems change in response to internal and external stimuli and evolve over time—they "learn" in that they adjust their behavior to the world around them. This chapter explores the threshold question of whether copyright systems, both physical and conceptual, might constitute complex adaptive systems.

To start with a very general proposition, the formation of systems appears to be an inherent feature in the universe. Interacting, interdependent elements create a unified whole—a system.[1] Modern science teaches that, from the moment of the Big Bang, the universe began to self-organize, forming layers of structure from the primordial soup: subatomic particles, atoms, molecules, right on up to planets, stars, and galaxies, all captured in the encompassing fabric of space-time.[2] Once life appeared, organisms evolved from single cells into a profusion of elaborate, multi-cellular creatures. In Darwin's words, "… from so simple a beginning endless forms most beautiful and most wonderful have been, and are being,

---

1 Merriam Webster's Collegiate Dictionary, 10th Ed., 1197 (1997).

2 Michael S. Turner, *Origin of the Universe*, Sci. Am., Sept. 2009, at 36.

evolved."[3] Systems may remain simple, with few parts engaged in mostly linear interactions, but most systems seem to evolve toward greater complexity. Discrete components, such as electrons or elephants, become part of larger systems, like atoms or herds. Those systems, in turn, become part of still greater systems such as elements and ecosystems.

Ecosystems and their constituent parts are paradigmatic complex adaptive systems. Many of the inhabitants of ecosystems are themselves complex adaptive systems. Humanity, at its current stage of evolution, both results from the evolution toward complex organization and contributes to it. Our own bodies are complex adaptive systems composed of complex adaptive systems such as the brain, the nervous system, and the immune system, which are themselves miniature ecosystems colonized by microbes. Like other animals, we inhabit natural ecosystems. We also collectively create complex social, political, economic, and legal systems in which we participate throughout our lives. As conscious beings, we attempt to control both natural and human-created complex adaptive systems.

Economists, political scientists, and sociologists have devoted considerable study to complexity in human systems. It may seem unlikely that diverse human and non-human systems could have much in common—that an ecosystem such as a prairie is really like an information system such as a publishing house. Complexity scholars in varied fields have, however, established that complex adaptive systems do share certain, general characteristics, whether the systems are natural or manmade. This chapter describes these characteristics, using examples taken from natural ecologies and from human systems, and then discusses similar characteristics displayed within the copyright system.

The Complexity Crash Course

Despite some variations in terminology across disciplines, there is general consensus on the essential properties of complex adaptive systems. For purposes of measuring the copyright system against these properties, they can be categorized as: intricate architecture, nonlinearity, emergence, and adaptiveness. As a result of these characteristics, the long-term behavior of complex adaptive systems is unpredictable and human attempts to intervene are likely to produce unanticipated consequences. The most sustainable complex systems maintain a state described as self-criticality or positioning at the "edge of chaos." The following discussion

---

3 Charles Darwin, The Origin of Species, quoted in Sean B. Carroll, Endless Forms Most Beautiful 282 (2005).

synthesizes, very much in lay terms, some basic principles of complexity drawn from a variety of sources.[4]

Architecture: Nests, Networks, and Loops

First, complex adaptive systems have a distinctive architecture. They typically contain many, heterogeneous elements, sometimes referred to as agents or actors. In a prairie, for example, herd animals, grasses, predators, and prey are all actors playing important roles in an ecosystem where biodiversity is critical to sustainability. In a market economy, regulatory organizations, financial institutions, corporate and individual producers, sellers, and buyers are all actors in the system. Complex adaptive systems often "nest" within each other so that the components of the primary system under observation are themselves complex adaptive systems that contain yet other complex adaptive systems. The prairie ecosystem includes the bison herds that include individual bison, each of which includes a brain, a nervous system, and so on. A market economy includes corporations and other institutions comprised of individual human beings, each of them composed of the complex adaptive systems of the human body. Thus, any agent, whether individual or institutional, is simultaneously involved in a multitude of complex adaptive systems, which overlap and interact with each other.

The constituent elements of each system tend to be densely interconnected in networks. Network connectivity enables the flow of information, money, products, energy, nutrients, or whatever other medium flows through the system. Consequently, actors within the system are directly or indirectly involved in interdependent relationships with other actors. Most direct interactions occur

---

4 The discussion of complexity in this chapter is synthesized from the following books: PER BAK, HOW NATURE WORKS: THE SCIENCE OF SELF-ORGANIZED CRITICALITY (1996); JOHN L. CASTI, COMPLEXIFICATION: EXPLAINING A PARADOXICAL WORLD THROUGH THE SCIENCE OF SURPRISE (1994); JAMES GLEICK, CHAOS: MAKING A NEW SCIENCE (1987); ROBERT JERVIS, SYSTEM EFFECTS: COMPLEXITY IN POLITICAL AND SOCIAL LIFE (1997); STEVEN JOHNSON, EMERGENCE: THE CONNECTED LIVES OF ANTS, BRAINS, CITIES, AND SOFTWARE (2001); STUART KAUFFMAN, AT HOME IN THE UNIVERSE: THE SEARCH FOR LAWS OF SELF-ORGANIZATION AND COMPLEXITY (1995); ROGER LEWIN, COMPLEXITY: LIFE AT THE EDGE OF CHAOS (1992); M. MITCHELL WALDROP, COMPLEXITY: THE EMERGING SCIENCE AT THE EDGE OF ORDER AND CHAOS (1992). With respect to complexity in legal systems, I have found particularly useful several articles by J. B. Ruhl, including the following: J. B. Ruhl, *Complexity Theory as a Paradigm for the Dynamical Law-And-Society System: A Wake-Up Call for Legal Reductionism and the Modern Administrative State,* 45 DUKE L.J. 849 (1996); J.B. Ruhl and Harold J. Ruhl, Jr., *The Arrow of the Law In Modern Administrative States: Using Complexity Theory to Reveal the Diminishing Returns and Increasing Risks the Burgeoning of Law Poses to Society*, 30 U.C. DAVIS L. REV. 405 (1997); J.B. Ruhl, *Law's Complexity: A Primer*, 24 GA. ST. U. L. REV. 885 (2008).

between neighboring actors, but the network interconnections assure that the effects of a change in conditions affecting one system element will be propagated throughout the system, often triggering cascades of further change. Where system elements are interdependent, change in one element may constrain or facilitate change in others.

Predators and prey on the prairie, for example, exist in interconnected food webs. If humans eradicate prairie dogs, coyotes will have to find alternate food sources or starve, and a responsive decline in predator populations may occur. The decrease of beneficial burrowing activities may also adversely impact the growth of grasses, thereby affecting the food supply and, hence, the survival of elk, bison, and other grazers. Market economies display similar interdependencies. The stock market is an enormous network of businesses and their investors, both individual and institutional, now supported by computer networks that facilitate instantaneous trading worldwide. The 2008 crash of the market as a result of risky investments in questionable financial instruments, and the resulting devastation to global economies, made painfully clear the interdependencies among investors, financial systems, and the overall health of market economies.

All of these interconnections contribute to a feature that straddles the divide between structure and behavior: the existence of feedback loops. Since complex adaptive systems are self-organizing, their interconnected architecture lays the groundwork for feedback and may then build new architecture along the feedback paths.[5] Denser interconnections create more feedback. Feedback may be positive or negative. In positive feedback, a change sets off reinforcing pressures that amplify change. Network effects, which cause the value of a good or service like an Internet connection to increase as more people use it, are a form of positive feedback. Positive feedback simply reinforces whatever change is occurring, whether that change is upward growth or a downward spiral. In negative feedback, a change triggers forces that counteract it and dampen the effects of change. A negative loop returns the system to approximately its original position in an attempt to keep the system in a stable condition known as homeostasis. Thermostats that respond to temperature changes by turning heating systems on or off to maintain a constant temperature are negative feedback devices. Traditional equilibrium economics assumes that price acts like a thermostat in the economy: if demand increases, price goes up, causing increases in supply, which causes price to fall until supply and demand are in balance.[6] Positive feedback loops contribute to instability; negative loops contribute to stability.

---

5 Ruhl, *Law's Complexity*, *supra* note 4, at 893.

6 *See* Eric. D. Beinhocker, The Origin of Wealth: Evolution, Complexity, and the Radical Remaking of Economics 109 (2006).

In predator–prey relationships, as the number of prey, like prairie dogs, increase, so do the number of predators, such as coyotes—a positive feedback loop. As coyotes grow too numerous, the prairie dog population declines which, in a negative feedback loop, causes a decrease in coyote populations. In a bullish stock market, the faith that value will increase creates positive feedback that encourages more investment, but the increasing cost of shares simultaneously produces negative feedback that deters some investors.[7] Recent events make clear that that positive feedback loops can push the markets down. The failure of important financial institutions in 2008 generated negative media coverage that made investors wary of further investments. As investment declined, stock prices dropped, starting a self-reinforcing downward spiral that continued until the market got so low that investors reentered the market to grab bargains.[8] Additionally, changes in one system not only feed back within that system, but they may cause change in interacting systems, which then feeds back to the primary system. Thus, the stock market drop quickly impacted economies around the world, drying up new development, causing business failures and job losses that, in turn, adversely impacted the stock market.

It is evident from the preceding examples that the effects of an agent's behavior also feed back to that agent, affecting its future behavior. Studies have shown that prey animals change their behavior in order to thwart predators.[9] Consumers caught short by the bursting of the housing bubble started saving more and buying less. Where system agents are human beings, they also try to anticipate the behavior of others, like the investors who reenter the market when they anticipate that the bottom has been reached.

Nonlinearity: Deterministic Rules, Butterfly Effects, and Path Dependence

Complex adaptive systems are dynamic and, not surprisingly given a networked structure typified by feedback loops, their processes are nonlinear in the long term. In linear systems, effects are proportional to causes. In nonlinear systems, effects are not necessarily proportional to their causes. In the case of the prairie dog and the coyote, the predator–prey relationship is not likely to be directly proportional

---

7 *See* W. Brian Arthur, *Complexity and the Economy*, 284 Science 107–109 (April 2, 1999), *available at* http://www.santafe.edu/arthur/Papers/Papers.html.

8 Robert J. Shiller, *An Echo Chamber of Boom and Bust*, N.Y. Times, August 29, 2009, at BU5.

9 Olivia Judson, *Where Tasty Morsels Fear to Tread*, N.Y. Times, Opinionator (Sept. 29, 2009; 10:11 PM), http://opinionator.blogs.nytimes.com/2009/09/29/where-tasty-morsels-fear-to-tread/.

because both species interact with other species and respond to many other factors in the ecosystem. In a market economy, stimulus spending should not foster merely an equal amount of production, but rather should kick-start businesses, forestall job losses, and, with luck, produce economic gains larger than the spending itself because of the diverse interactions between elements of supply and demand in the economy.

Complex adaptive systems do follow defined, deterministic rules that, in the short term, produce relatively predictable behaviors. Ant colonies operate under rules in which pheromone trails communicate vital information about such important topics as food locations or imminent threats. Bison herds follow established patterns in mating and migration. In human-constructed systems, we consciously set many of the rules of interaction. Actors in market economies follow accepted rules set by domestic laws, international treaties, and commercial and social norms. However, because of the networked interdependencies and feedback loops among system actors, a change at one point cascades unpredictably throughout the system producing chaotic behavior.

In the complexity lexicon, "chaotic" does not mean "random." Chaotic systems follow deterministic rules of interaction, but when those rules are followed in the aggregate, they result in unpredictable behavior or "deterministic randomness." John Casti provides the following example of deterministic randomness: a saltwater taffy–pulling machine repeatedly performs the same mechanical function; however, two raisins initially placed very close together in the taffy will over time end up in dramatically different positions and it is impossible to predict their future, relative positions. The rule of action, taffy pulling, is deterministic, but the results are unpredictable.[10] Meteorologists know a great deal about the rules guiding planetary weather systems, yet they can rarely predict the weather more than a day or two in advance. Those systems produce the storms whose lightning sets prairies ablaze at entirely unpredictable times, producing beneficial, indeed essential, ecosystem effects by clearing out old growth and making way for new. Financial markets follow accepted rules, yet the unexpected demise of Lehmann Brothers engendered panic among investors and sent the stock market into a tailspin.

Systems exhibiting chaotic behavior are described as "sensitive to initial conditions." A tiny change in the initial conditions to which a system responds can produce wide divergences in system development. Certain patterns may recur but never in exactly the same way because initial conditions will have changed. This

10 Casti, *supra* note 4, at 91–2.

phenomenon is popularly known as the "butterfly effect." A butterfly flapping its wings in the Amazon rain forest may, on one occasion, set off a chain of events in the atmosphere that, a month later, produces a tornado in Oklahoma. On a different occasion, the butterfly's actions may have no effect at all. The butterfly example, which exists in many variations, demonstrates two aspects of nonlinearity: (1) very small actions may have very large consequences, and (2) even slight changes in initial conditions may produce very different outcomes. For actors in a particular system, sensitivity to initial conditions means that their very actions change the conditions of the system so that the same action, taken at a later point in time, may not produce the same result. A small investment in Apple stock when its price is low (a rare occurrence in recent years) may be part of a wave of such investments that produces gains as the stock goes up. The exact same investment made at a later time may produce no gain at all or even a loss dependent on many other factors affecting Apple stocks.

Sensitivity to initial conditions means that complex adaptive systems are path dependent. They have a history that influences their future trajectories; future options may be limited by past choices. New architecture may form along a chosen path so that changes in the system "lock in" and prove difficult to reverse. For example, complexity economists studying technology markets have suggested that an initial advantage for a technology or standard may, because of sensitivity to initial conditions and historical "lock-in," have adverse effects even in free markets. They offer the example of the QWERTY keyboard, which became the industry standard because the large majority of keyboard users learned to type on the QWERTY system and resisted learning another system.[11] In the environment, a species like the bison may adapt so completely to a particular niche that it cannot re-adapt quickly enough to survive environmental change. In financial markets, financial deregulation permitted the growth of financial architectures that made some companies "too big to fail" without taking the global economic system with them. Opinions differ over the true "irreversibility" of path-dependent behavior—after all, the bison were saved, financial institutions can be re-regulated—but, at

[11] Economists differ over whether such technological path dependence is irreversible. *Compare* W. Brian Arthur, *Positive Feedbacks in the Economy*, 262 Sci. Am. 92–9, Feb. 1990, and *Competing Technologies, Increasing Returns, and Lock-In by Historical Events*, 99 Econ. J. 116–31 (March 1989), *available at* http://www.santafe.edu/arthur/Papers/Pdf_files/EJ.pdf, *with* S.J. Liebowitz and Stephen Margolis, *Path Dependence, Lock-In, and History,* 11 J. L. Econ. & Org. 205 (Apr. 1995), *available at* http://www.utdallas.edu/~liebowit/paths.html.

a minimum, path dependence creates resistance to change; at maximum, it may foreclose some options.

Emergence: Self-organized, Systemic Patterns

Against this resistance to change must be set the quality of emergence, the indispensible characteristic of all complex adaptive systems. The aggregated behavior of system actors following simple rules of interaction produces unexpected, system-wide patterns and behavior that may have no clear relationship to a particular actor or rule. Rather, the system as a whole develops cooperative, shared behaviors. One cannot simply add the constituent elements of the system together to predict behavior since interactions among the elements, and in response to external conditions, produce system behavior unlike the individual behavior of each element. The system as a whole is not just more than the sum of its parts; it is different than the sum of its parts.

The complex division of labor that emerges in an ant colony is a collective behavior quite different from the simple rules followed by single ants. The queen does not direct this activity; rather the colony or hive as a whole develops a "swarm logic" that prioritizes between food sources and switches workers among activities such as nest building or foraging. The microbehaviors of individual ants produce macrobehaviors at the higher level of the colony as a whole. The flock of birds wheeling and diving in perfect unison above the prairie in a clear autumn sky represents emergence in action as does the direction and flow of a running bison herd. Many neuroscientists believe that consciousness is an emergent property of the brain. Nor are such patterns limited to biological life. Weather systems create emergent patterns in the form of tornados, hurricanes, and similar phenomena. Ocean and air currents contain hidden structures.[12] Repetitive, irregular fractal patterns appear in tree branches, leaves, lightning, shorelines, seashells, and any number of other natural phenomena.

The aggregate activities of human beings also produce emergent properties. Laws, social norms, and customs emerge as necessary elements of social and political self-organization. Research has debunked the myth of true anarchism even in pirate communities and the American "Wild West"; in both situations, participants spontaneously created their own institutions and codes of behavior.[13] In cities, we form neighborhoods, even in the absence of conscious city planning.

[12] Bina Venkataraman, *Finding Order in the Apparent Chaos of Currents*, N.Y.Times, Sept. 29, 2009, at D1.

[13] Michael Shermer, *Captain Hook meets Adam Smith*, Sci. Am., Oct. 2009, at 34.

On the World Wide Web and the Internet, patterns of linkage and traffic appear. Emergent behaviors, from fashion trends to passing fads, form much of the constant ebb and flow of human cultural life.

For better or worse, as individuals coalesce to form collectives like government bureaucracies or business corporations, those entities often come to exhibit behaviors quite different from those of the individuals that compose them. The interests and actions of workers in manufacturing industries, for example, may actually be adverse to the corporate course set by management—hence the development of unions. At higher levels, these institutions become part of even larger collectives: the economy, the government, the society, and the legal system. Perhaps the most familiar emergent property in a large collectivity is Adam Smith's "invisible hand." The aggregate activity of businesses, financial markets, and consumers selfishly pursuing their own self-interests in the marketplace, with no regard for the general welfare, theoretically produces the optimal benefit to society as a whole as if orchestrated by an invisible hand. Similarly, through the self-serving actions of investors, stock markets regulate the value of companies, producing trends upward or downward without any central director. Prices are an emergent property of markets.

Emergent properties can be either good or bad from a normative standpoint. They have no moral compass. They are simply responses to conditions in the system and its surrounding environment. Weather systems may produce climates conducive to agriculture, but also produce tornados and hurricanes as emergent behaviors. Emergent patterns in political and economic systems may produce Hitler and Stalin as readily as Washington and Jefferson. Risky investments by financial institutions were part of a pattern of emergent behavior recently produced by the financial system as a result of the self-interested actions of millions of homeowners, banks, and individual and institutional investors, aided and abetted by inactive regulators who erroneously assumed that all emergent properties of markets were good.

Emergent properties naturally result from the diverse, interconnected structures and dynamic processes occurring in a complex adaptive system as a whole. Emergent patterns also feed back into the system, causing further changes in an adaptive cycle. Consequently, emergent patterns cannot be predicted based solely on knowledge about individual system components or the local rules of interaction that they follow. Traditional reductive analysis will not produce an adequate understanding of the system as a whole. In addition, reductive analysis of one system is apt to miss important roles played by other complex adaptive systems.

Adaptiveness: Coevolution and Punctuated Equilibria

Complex adaptive systems evolve over time not only in response to their own internal dynamics, but also in response to other systems. Biological species develop morphologies and behaviors that favor their survival within the ecosystems they inhabit. Markets respond to changes in consumer tastes, new technologies, the cost and availability of raw materials, and numerous other factors. In essence, complex adaptive systems "learn" from their environments. They incorporate their experiences in schema, such as DNA for biological species, or institutions, customs, and laws for human societies.

Some adaptations may be instigated by entirely exogenous events. For example, current science suggests that the ecosystems inhabited by the dinosaurs were destroyed by a comet impact which forced all existing species to either adapt, as mammal ancestors did, or die out, as the dinosaurs did. Such overwhelming catastrophes are infrequent. Most adaptation results from co-evolution with other systems since the environment to which a given system responds consists primarily of other systems. The prairie dog, for example, evolved in an environment composed of many other systems including the climate, prairie flora, and other prairie fauna, some of which prey on prairie dogs. Economies coevolve with social, technological, political, and legal systems. Changes in one system spark changes in those with which it interacts, producing further adaptations. In predator–prey webs, an adaptation giving the prey an advantage will initiate a "coupled" adaptation in the predator. If the prairie dog becomes faster, it forces the coyote to become faster, or find other prey, or face extinction. If the stock market tanks, its impacts are felt throughout the economy as related systems, such as businesses and consumers, respond to the new financial environment.

Coevolving systems follow a typical evolutionary pattern consisting of long stable periods interrupted by swift change as the system reaches a tipping point at which change becomes inevitable. Ecologists and evolutionary biologists describe this pattern as "punctuated equilibrium." The Cambrian explosion of multicellular life forms following eons dominated by unicellular forms serves as the paradigm of a biological punctuation.[14] Economies noticeably exhibit repetitive fluctuations, such as stock market crashes and recessions. Civilizations have risen, flourished for centuries, and then fallen into disarray. Periods of rapid change involve innovation and experimentation with new forms, followed by a severe winnowing of less successful forms and increased specialization. In the Cambrian era, for example, an enormous variety of body forms appeared, most of which subsequently went

---

14 *See* Lewin, *supra* note 4, at 100–101.

extinct, leaving the smaller range of body forms from which modern organisms are built. A similar pattern of innovation appears in ancient civilizations like the Anasazi and modern industries like the automobile industry.[15]

Unpredictability and the Edge of Chaos

The behavior of systems characterized by intricate architecture, nonlinearity, emergence, and adaptability will be unpredictable over the long term. Human involvement in complex adaptive systems produces enhanced potential for unexpected outcomes because humans consciously seek to control systems that affect them, whether those systems are natural or human-created. We exploit, and may destroy, ecosystems for purposes of survival or to amass wealth. We create laws and other rules to shape the courses of social, political, and economic systems. Such interventions may produce short-term predictability in day-to-day interactions. Indeed, laws and norms are meant to engender consistency. Over the long term, though, they may produce unintended consequences as responses ripple through the system. In free markets, a growing economy may be the unintended result of the pursuit of self-interest in the marketplace. We have recently learned, to our detriment, that deregulatory measures intended to amplify that effect may, on the contrary, lead to financial catastrophe, the unanticipated consequence. How, then, should we approach the regulation of complex adaptive systems? The concept of the "edge of chaos" suggests that the goal of human intervention in such systems should be to find a productive balance between order and chaos.

Complex adaptive behavior occurs in a border area between ordered and chaotic behaviors — "a "no-man's land" in which chaos and stability pull in opposite directions."[16] Complexity researchers refer to this area as "the edge of chaos" or self organized criticality. The variance in terminology derives from different fields of research, but both refer to systems perched at the point of transition from one state to another. Complex adaptive systems find an internal balance between linear, predictable behaviors and nonlinear, unpredictable behaviors. They evolve and coevolve toward the edge of chaos, which provides them with both the stability required for self-maintenance and the flexibility to adapt to changing circumstances. Prairie ecosystems comprise a complex system of relationships between flora and fauna, climate and weather, capable of enduring for thousands of years despite fluctuations in predator–prey populations, drought and flood, fire and regrowth. Economic history affirms that neither centrally

[15] *Id.*, at 18, 70–71.

[16] Lewin, *supra* note 4, at 51.

planned communist economies nor complete laissez-faire economies are optimal. The most dynamic, sustainable economies find a balance between innovation and regulation. The balance between order and chaos may shift from time to time and require adjustment, but the most robust, sustainable systems seek it out.

One hallmark of systems at the "edge" is the "power law distribution." When perturbed, such systems produce a probabilistic range of responses in which big responses are rare and small ones are frequent. Studies of earthquake distributions show, for example, that fault zones do not build pressure until they slip catastrophically, but rather approach the point of slippage, then undergo a steady succession of slips of various magnitudes that serve to keep the tension at the critical point until, eventually, a major earthquake occurs. Power law distributions have been found in many human systems, such as stock market fluctuations and traffic patterns.[17] A system operating with such a distribution has the resilience to survive environmental changes up to a point. However, as the earthquake distribution suggests, if pushed hard enough it will reach a "tipping point" and topple over the edge into a fundamentally new state. The long lists of extinct species and defunct civilizations bear witness to the fact that complex adaptive systems can fail. Prairie ecosystems could not survive widespread farming. Markets can crash, as they did during the Great Depression, and came perilously close to doing in the past few years. They are replaced by other systems more suited to the changed environment, typically a different set of complex adaptive systems exhibiting the characteristic structures and behaviors of such systems.

Is Copyright Complex?

If the information ecosystem is a complex adaptive system, it should demonstrate the characteristics outlined above. If the subset of the information ecosystem affected by copyrights—the copyright ecosystem—is a complex adaptive system, it too will demonstrate them. Copyright involves concrete, physical systems like copyright-related industries, government agencies such as the Copyright Office, law firms and lawyers that specialize in copyright, and so on. It also includes the conceptual system of copyright law that sets some of the rules by which other copyright systems operate. Do these overlapping systems possess the structure and behavior typical of complex adaptive systems? An overview of these systems suggests they fit comfortably within the standard complexity mold.

---

[17] *See, e.g.*, Bak, *supra* note 4, at 183–98.

Architecture

As the brief tour in the previous chapter illustrates, the copyright ecosystem shares the intricate architecture common to complex adaptive systems—in this case, an architecture rapidly changing in response to new technologies. The ecosystem contains numerous, diverse actors. Authors, publishers, movie studios, and other creators produce a tremendous variety of copyrightable works in an equally wide variety of analog and digital media. They distribute their works through complex networks to millions of institutional and individual buyers and users. Those networks include both commercial channels and noncommercial distributors like lending libraries or educational institutions. Increasingly, the legal channels are supplemented by user distribution through illicit channels like social or file sharing networks.

Many, if not most, of the actors in the copyright universe display the typical nesting pattern of complex adaptive systems: multinational corporate entities, composed of subsidiaries, composed of individual employees who are, of course, human beings composed of the usual complex human systems. They obviously interact with broader economic, legal, social, and political systems. Technology companies develop some products that affect copyrighted material, but may also develop other kinds of technologies not related to copyright. Social networks share, and create, copyrighted works but also serve many other purposes. Courts decide copyright cases, but also decide many other kinds of cases. Thus the copyright "ecosystem" contains many subsystems which may themselves be complex adaptive systems.

Resources flow through the networks that connect this large cast of copyright actors: information in the form of works and market information, money (lots of money), and the copyright rights themselves, which can be legally transferred among actors through contractual agreements. The various institutional and individual agents in the system are interdependent. Warner Brothers could not produce the Harry Potter movies without J.K. Rowling's novels. There would be no movie soundtrack recordings, posters, or dolls of the stars without the movies. None of it could succeed without consumers willing to pay, and pay handsomely, for the works. Similar interdependencies exist in other copyright subsystems: the relationships among recording studios, radio stations, their artists, their fans, and entertainment media, for example, or among television networks, producers of television shows, actors, entertainment media, and fans. Obviously, many of these interconnections are feedback loops.

Works flow out from producers; money and information about consumer preferences flows back in, to be used by producers in plotting their future strategies. In the case of the Potter books, the enormous positive feedback loop from readers created a publishing phenomenon which then set off a movie phenomenon, a merchandising bonanza, and so on. Similar feedback loops produce hit songs, movies, and television shows or superstar musicians, actors, and comedians. Producers of copyrighted works alter their behavior in anticipation of consumer responses. Spinoffs and sequels in the same or different media are common responses to positive feedback. Cancellations and the remainder bins are responses to the lack thereof.

In addition, actors in the copyright ecosystem are affected by feedbacks from the larger environment. As significant players in the national economies, particularly in developed nations, the copyright industries are as fully impacted by economic change as other businesses. In some cases, bad news for the economy may even be good news for copyright industries like movie studios that have historically prospered during economic downturns. Copyright industries also feel the impact of feedback from technological innovations affecting content delivery and use. Development of technologies of dissemination forces change in the way copyrighted works are created, distributed, and used. The formation of social networks whose members exchange works has significant impact on copyright industries.

With respect to copyright law in particular, the physical law-related constituents of the copyright system include, among others: the legislative bodies around the world that craft domestic copyright law and international treaties; the law firms who craft the agreements among copyright agents; the courts that decide disputes over copyright ownership. These institutions display the typical nesting pattern of complex adaptive systems. The formation of copyright law demonstrates extensive feedback loops. Relatively simple early statutes accumulate judicial and academic interpretations that gradually elaborate both the theory and doctrine of copyright. Legislators then incorporate that feedback into the statutes, instigating a new loop of interpretations and elaborations that gradually change the corpus of the law. Both the statutes and their interpretations also respond to feedback from other systems, such as technology systems and markets. As a result of that feedback, the law has gradually come to encompass not merely traditional print media, but the whole host of analog and digital media developed after the initial creation of copyright law. Architecturally, then, the copyright ecosystem does exhibit the intricate, networked, looping structure typical of complex adaptive systems.

Nonlinearity

Such intricate structures inevitably contribute to nonlinear behaviors in the long term, despite our attempts to formulate legal rules of action in copyright systems that will produce linear, predictable effects. Actors in the copyright ecosystem follow many of the same rules followed in the economy at large, with the notable addition of copyright law, the basic rule set delineating the rights of copyright holders. Copyright law is far from simple, but its basic requirements are well known to commercial players in the system and keep most transactions predictable in the short term. However, the transition to electronic media has clearly introduced elements of chaos into the system despite the rules.

As one example of a clearly nonlinear effect, consider the impact of Shawn Fanning and Napster on the copyright industries. A lone programmer, tinkering with software for his own benefit and that of his music loving buddies, produces the first successful peer-to-peer (P2P) file sharing software and thereby sets off massive cascading changes that, in fairly short order, produce drastic disruptions in the sound recording industry and threaten numerous other copyright industries. P2P was the butterfly that set off the tornado. Changes in technologies of dissemination, from moveable type through the World Wide Web, have repeatedly set off such disruptions in copyright systems.

Copyright systems also are demonstrably sensitive to initial conditions as demonstrated by the inability of producers to assure favorable outcomes even for very similar works. Sequels, prequels, remakes, and spinoffs can be viewed as conscious attempts to recapture the conditions that created past successes. Yet they fail as often as they succeed. The history of movie remakes bears witness to this fact of complex life. The 1949 film *All the King's Men* won multiple Oscars and is a recognized classic; the 2006 remake was a commercial and critical failure. Hitchcock's 1960 "Psycho" was a classic; the 1998 remake a bomb. Sequels and spinoffs recycling popular stories abound; some succeed, some fail. The dominance of such recycled products in modern culture reflects yet another characteristic of complex adaptive systems: path dependence.

The copyright ecosystem is relatively young compared to environmental ecosystems or other human systems like market economies. Yet it shows signs of path dependence, both institutionally and legally. As new copyright industries emerge, they build architectures of production and distribution that can be hard to dismantle if the business climate changes. In particular, copyright holders have a long history of resistance to new technologies including the photocopier, the videotape recorder, and now digital media. The sound recording industry and its associated distribution systems offer a recent example of path dependence by one copyright subsystem. The industry built a bricks-and-mortar system appropriate for distribution of physical copies in a non-networked world. That system became a liability once the Internet enabled online sales of physical and electronic copies. The industry, committed to its old path, resisted online distribution until overwhelming economic forces destroyed much of the physical distribution network. The studios' long adherence to the old path crippled them in the networked economy. Ironically, their inflexibility provided the window of opportunity for the development and popularization of peer-to-peer technologies that continue to devastate their revenue streams. Other established copyright industries now face similar problems as their established business models are challenged by, and offer resistance to, new technologies.

Path dependence also appears in copyright law. As copyright industries gained economic power, their influence produced a definite path in copyright law toward enactment of stronger copyright protection for more kinds of works for longer periods of time. Copyright holders successfully pursued the linear argument that, if copyright protection incentivizes creation, more copyright protection must surely result in more production of creative works. Thus, protections originally devised only for books, maps, and charts now extend to an astounding variety of works in many different media, from the fine arts to software. Copyright's duration has lengthened substantially. Yet, if the copyright ecosystem as a whole is complex and adaptive, its nonlinear behaviors mean that the proposition that more copyright protection must produce more creativity cannot be taken for granted. There are too many factors in play.

The legal system is famously path dependent, building new law incrementally from old law by case decision and statutory amendment. In common law, the doctrine of *stare decisis* constrains courts to follow established judicial precedents. In civil law, judges do not follow *stare decisis* but are, nonetheless, expected to interpret law in a predictable manner under the principle of *jurisprudence constante*. Copyright law has followed this path for several centuries, becoming a conceptual system of daunting scope and complication. Once new protections are written into copyright law, they are rarely elided by subsequent enactment. Thus, a provision drafted to create a compulsory license for player piano rolls may come to govern later developed media like sound recordings.[18] Notwithstanding recent

[18] 17 U.S.C. § 115 (2006) created a compulsory license for sound recordings of musical compositions. Congress intended the provision merely to forestall a monopoly on piano rolls, but it ultimately influenced the development of the entire sound recording industry. *See* William W. Fisher III, Promises to Keep 48–9 (2004).

calls by some commentators for the complete abandonment of copyright for works like sound recordings, copyright's historical path makes it extremely unlikely that copyright laws will disappear any time soon despite emergent phenomena challenging both the law and existing copyright industries.

Emergence

The copyright ecosystem provides examples of self-organization and emergence both as a whole and in its various subsystems. Its architecture and legal rules developed in concert with parallel developments in markets for content and technologies of reproduction and distribution. The first copyright law emerged from the turmoil caused by the invention of the printing press. The emergence of copyright law initialized the formal copyright system by defining legally protectable rights in certain kinds of works. That protection enhanced the ability of copyright-based industries to attain the economic and political power that they subsequently exercised to expand the scope of copyright law—a formidable feedback effect.

Copyright industries have spontaneously organized or reorganized with every change in information technologies. As each technology appears, new organizations emerge to take advantage of the combination of copyrightable content with the new medium. The invention of radio and television sparked the emergence of the broadcast industries. The film industry coalesced around the movie camera. More recent developments like computer animation, video game technologies, and the Internet, have generated their own emergent organizations. Many of these organizations obviously take the familiar forms common to other economic actors, such as partnerships, corporations, and conglomerates, customized for the production and dissemination of copyrightable content. Electronic technologies, on the other hand, have also sparked the emergence of unusual kinds of collectives like wikis and blogs that may or may not be structured in traditional economic forms or operate in accordance with traditional copyright law.

With the advent of each new medium, new legal rules have emerged to regularize transactions involving new forms of copyrighted content and the industries that produce them. The formulation of these rules is particularly "emergent" in nature, thanks to a longstanding practice by which key industries often participate in the actual drafting of copyright laws. As copyright players pursue their interests through litigation, courts also add new variations, or even entirely new doctrines, to the corpus of copyright law. New and revised copyright rules may bubble up from the industries and through the judiciary before Congress imposes them top down by writing them into the statute, as they did in the lengthy revision process that produced the current Copyright Act.

Perhaps the most significant emergent pattern to appear recently in the digital copyright ecosystem is a strong norm favoring free sharing of copyrightable works among thousands of consumers through P2P and social networks. An enhanced sharing norm supported by new technologies has also emerged among creators. Cooperation, collaboration, and collectivism are catchphrases for the technorati, and the line between creator and consumer is increasingly blurry. Aggregator sites for communities of interest allow users to share, label, classify, and use pools of information. Yahoo and Google together host over 10 million such interest groups.[19] The Open Source movement, which uses contract law in the form of licenses to encourage shared development of software programs, first established a model for peer production. Now wiki software enables organized collective projects like Wikipedia.

Sharing behavior, as such, is not new. Humans are the most social of all species and have undoubtedly shared cultural artifacts from the moment they began to form the social groups that proved to be one of the keys to their evolutionary success. Artists have collaborated with one another from the first cave painting right down to the present day. In fact, copyright owners have always profited from this proclivity for sharing. Consumers spread the word about their favorite works, creating the "buzz" that pumps up the sales of the most successful works and their derivatives. What has changed, dramatically, is their capacity to share not merely the "buzz" but the complete content of copyrighted works without payment to the copyright holder. The emergence of sharing norms that extend beyond family and friends to thousands of complete strangers connected by nothing more than Internet access presents an enormous challenge to the copyright system as a whole. It must either coevolve with new technologies, and the social and economic networks they enable, or face extinction.

Adaptiveness

The copyright ecosystem clearly interacts with many other systems including technology industries, political institutions, social networks, legal institutions, and markets and has evolved in concert with them. Over time, it has become a behemoth encompassing a tremendous amount of cultural content and populated

---

[19] Kevin Kelly, *The New Socialism: Global Collectivist Society is Coming Online*, WIRED, Vol. 17.06, May 22, 2009, *available at* http://www.wired.com/culture/culturereviews/magazine/17-06/nep_newsocialism.

by industries that wield considerable political and economic power. Content providers adapt their products to changes in customer tastes and customers, in turn, change their purchasing patterns in response to new products, and marketing thereof, by providers. Both providers and customers respond to changes that may be instigated by competitors, to economic factors, and to new technologies such as e-book readers or iPads. The system now faces major dislocations caused by what may be the first true punctuation in its relatively short evolution: the shift from analog to digital media.

The copyright ecosystem successfully absorbed innovations in analog technologies with minor disruption despite recurrent claims that new technologies tolled the death knell of established industries: that television and, later, the videotape recorder would kill the movie industry, for example, or that cassette tapes would wipe out the recording studios. New analog technologies more often added new sources of revenue for the copyright holders; the system simply incorporated new formats and continued to grow. Starting in the mid-1990s when Internet use by ordinary consumers surged exponentially, the combination of cheap, perfect digital copying technologies with global connectivity forced the system as a whole to a punctuation point whose effects are still unfolding. The digital transition, for the first time, challenged the bedrock copyright notion that the value can be extracted from works by controlling relatively expensive physical copies moving through physical distribution channels. Experimentation with new forms is widespread.

Copyright-related industries have always experimented with new forms for conveying content, winnowing out the less successful or simply outgrowing them as new technologies developed. Software developers, for example, experimented with different formats, winnowing them down to a few interoperable standards, and then making incremental improvements to those standards. Competing videotape formats (Betamax and Video Home System [VHS]) were narrowed down to a single standard, as were competing formats for high definition (HD) movie media (HD and Blu-ray). Different e-book formats still contend with one another. Experimentation has produced digital rights management (DRM) systems, password-protected online subscription systems, distribution of physical copies through online sellers like Amazon.com, direct electronic delivery through a variety of online channels, and numerous other features of the digital marketplace for copyrighted works.

The industries are not the only system actors engaged in experimentation. Authors in different media experiment with collective creation, direct online distribution, print-on-demand, and new business models in which free content is combined with sales of physical objects. Consumers continue to interact with a wide variety of Web sites offering content and with every new technology that offers them the ability to share works of their own or copyrighted works. What will survive such ferment is still an open question, but we have already seen, for example, Google surge ahead of Yahoo, Facebook outpace MySpace, early e-book formats displaced by the Kindle and the iPad, hard copy newspapers displaced by online news sites and blogs.

Copyright law as a conceptual system has also evolved in response to digitization as powerful industries seek stronger protections, not only in the form of expanded scope and duration of copyright laws, but also in the form of paracopyright laws like the Digital Millennium Copyright Act (DMCA), which prohibits circumvention of copyright protection technologies and creates safe harbors for online service providers. The World Intellectual Property Organization (WIPO) has formulated new model treaties that attempt to meet the challenges of the digital age.[20] The TRIPs agreement attempts to strengthen copyright globally by tying it to trade. In the meantime, creators also experiment with tweaking copyright law through open source licenses or outright abandonment of copyright rights. Such widespread experimentation with legal approaches raises the specter of a different law: the law of unintended consequences.

Unpredictability and the Edge of Chaos

Certainly, the copyright ecosystem has always been capable of producing unexpected behavior. The digital challenge has, if anything, amped up the degree of unpredictability. What average citizen would have predicted as little as 10 years ago that Apple would become the dominant distributor of recorded music? Or that cellular phones would become major repositories for content like games and movies as well as handy gadgets for voice communication? In an unpredictable system, intervention will produce unintended consequences. The recording industry's legal assault on file sharers, while it produced favorable court outcomes, did nothing to stop the industry's losses, but instead produced a public relations backlash that may have contributed to the growth of file sharing. The Digital Millennium Copyright Act,[21] intended to prevent unauthorized access to copyrighted works, has markedly failed to stop either commercial piracy or file

---

20 *See* the WIPO Copyright Treaty, Dec. 20, 1996, and WIPO Performances And Phonograms Treaty, Dec. 20, 1996, *available at* http://www.wipo.int/treaties/en/ip/wct/trtdocs_wo033.html#P87_12240 and http://www.wipo.int/treaties/en/ip/wppt/trtdocs_wo034.html, respectively.

21 17 U.S.C. § 512, 1201–5 (2006).

sharing but has, instead, been used on several occasions to scare security experts out of revealing flaws in encryption systems or in attempts to protect monopolies in replacement parts.[22] Consequently, whether copyright law can be used effectively to keep the copyright ecosystem as a whole sustainable is an open question.

The copyright ecosystem has certainly shown considerable resilience over its 300-year history, riding out the smaller shocks presented by new technologies of reproduction up until the digital revolution. The power law distributions typical of self-criticality are evident in the historic distribution of hits and misses in copyright industries. The blockbuster success is rare, the failure or moderate success far more common. If, however, digitization represents a punctuation point in the system's evolution, it may be too soon to tell whether the system is or can remain at the edge of chaos in the face of a sea change in its environment.

Conclusion

The copyright ecosystem, in its varied aspects, certainly displays the characteristic behaviors of complex adaptive systems like natural ecosystems: complex architecture, nonlinearity, emergence, adaptiveness, and unpredictability. Publishing houses and other copyright systems do indeed behave, in many ways, like prairies and other ecosystems. Admittedly, the examples of such behavior are anecdotal, rather than the result of exhaustive empirical analysis, but they are pervasive. Comparisons of prairies to publishers do not prove that the copyright ecosystem and its many subsystems are all complex adaptive systems. Rather they support a hypothesis to that effect and suggest that these systems ought to be studied more closely within a complexity framework. The "information ecosystem" meme may well be more than a convenient analogy.

Copyright law is generally viewed as the primary vehicle through which we intervene to create an environment conducive to creative production. It would seem to be axiomatic that if we are to succeed in that endeavor, we must understand the workings of the system in order to calibrate laws that will encourage creativity. Like the prairie ecosystem or a free market economy, the copyright ecosystem can be approached as a complex adaptive system composed of many complex adaptive subsystems that can be studied empirically. Copyright researchers can study the system's constituent parts, processes, and interdependencies just as ecologists

22 *See* Lexmark v. Static Control Components, 387 F.3d 522 (6th cir. 2004) (printer cartridges) and Chamberlain v. Skylink, 381 F.3d 1178 (Fed. Cir. 2004) (garage door openers).

map out the elements and relationships of a prairie ecosystem. Empirical research would provide a basis for decisions about how, or if, we should intervene to guide the future evolution of the copyright system. Moreover, if the copyright system is complex and adaptive, it must seek the edge of chaos in order to be sustainable, and the most effective laws would seek to keep the system poised on that edge. Complexity models that acknowledge the inherent characteristics of complex adaptive systems should help legislators design, and judges interpret, better copyright laws that are more likely to achieve the goals for which copyright laws were first created.

Unfortunately, beyond the generally accepted statement that copyright should encourage creativity, the exact goals and theoretical justifications offered for copyright's existence are not entirely clear or consistent. Until quite recently, few researchers have subjected either physical copyright institutions or copyright laws to rigorous empirical analysis. Empirical information has rarely guided copyright lawmaking. Rather, most copyright law emerges from a legislative process in which industry lobbyists skillfully manipulate raw political influence and several antiquated philosophical theories to achieve, if that is the word, compromises that favor their business interests. Consequently, we must temporarily step back from the cutting edge of complexity theory to consider the history and philosophical underpinnings of copyright, before we can consider the ways in which complexity theory might offer a substantially more useful theoretical framework for copyright.

Chapter 2
A Philosopher and a Lobbyist Walk into a Bar: The Theory and Reality of Copyright Lawmaking

Sadly, the title of this chapter is not the opening line of a joke. It would be more accurate, at least in the United States (U.S.), if the philosopher and the lobbyist walked directly into a legislative chamber or a round of trade negotiations and began drafting laws based on the philosopher's speculations and the lobbyist's wish list. The first copyright law, enacted at the request of English publishers, actually predates the development of the theoretical justifications now commonly offered for copyright's existence. After-the-fact philosophizing, however, laid the groundwork for industry lobbyists intent on securing maximum copyright protection. While all legislation is subject to influence from lobbyists for powerful industries, copyright legislation succumbed earlier and more completely than most to such influence, abetted by legislative abdication of responsibility for the arcane, complicated body of law that so mystifies consumers and, it sometimes seems, legislators themselves. This chapter provides a very brief history of copyright law and its theoretical justifications and points out a few problems produced by the unfortunate confluence of political influence and philosophy in the making of copyright law.

A Brief History

The Statute of Anne and its Successors

The Statute of Anne, adopted by the English Parliament in 1709, effective in 1710, was the first copyright law.[1] The precursor of the Statute was a true monopoly granted by the Crown in 1557 to the Stationer's Company, a trade guild for printers, booksellers (publishers), and bookbinders. The invention of the printing press in the mid-1400's enabled the formation of the businesses represented by the Stationer's Company. It also threatened the dominant political system, the Crown, with dissemination of subversive materials, particularly those associated

---

1 Statute of Anne, 1710, 8 Ann., c.19 (Eng.).

with the bloody religious strife of the period. The Crown addressed the problem by chartering a perpetual publishing monopoly to the Stationer's Company, which happily exercised the function of censorship on the Crown's behalf. As continued by subsequent renewals and licensing acts, the monopoly persisted for more than a century and a half.[2]

By the early 1700's, the Crown's need to suppress dissenting religious views had waned, and the high costs of the perpetual monopoly had stoked resentment against the Stationers. When the Licensing Acts expired, the Stationers lobbied for passage of a new law to perpetuate their monopoly. The old argument that a press monopoly was essential to good governance fell on deaf ears, so the publishers shifted ground, arguing that copyright protection was necessary to protect authors and their assigns, such as publishers. In a classic case of unanticipated consequences, they got a law rather different from the one they desired. The Statute of Anne, for the first time, recognized the rights of authors, not publishers, to control the reproduction of their works. In order to thwart the Stationers' dreams of monopoly, the drafters limited coverage to new books newly published and limited the duration of protection to14 years with an author's right of renewal for the same period. No protection existed prior to publication or after expiration of the copyright, at which point the work went into the public domain, available for all to use.

The Statute of Anne was essentially a trade regulation pragmatically designed to prevent the recurrence of expensive, perpetual publishing monopolies, whose evils had become apparent under the old monopoly. It benefited authors, limited publisher overreaching, and protected the public domain. It was not the product of elaborate theories of ownership rights, but a clever solution to an existing problem. The elaborate theorizing first appeared in the context of publisher lawsuits. After Parliament rejected publishers' attempts to revitalize their old, perpetual rights, the publishers turned to the courts, claiming that the source of the author's copyright was natural law not the positive law, with all its limitations, enacted by the Statute.

Initially, the publishers succeeded in convincing the court in *Millar v. Taylor*[3] that the author had a perpetual common law right under natural law that could be assigned to the publisher, also in perpetuity. Had that decision stood, the Stationers' monopoly would have been back in business. The House of Lords overruled Millar five years later in *Donaldson v. Beckett*,[4] holding that the author's common law

---

2 The history of the Statute of Anne summarized herein is recounted at length in L. Ray Patterson and Stanley F. Birch, Jr., *A Unified Theory of Copyright* (Craig Joyce, ed., 2009), 46 Hous. L. Rev. 215, 244–56 (2009).

3 98 Eng. Rep. 201 (1769).

4 1 Eng. Rep. 837 (H.L. 1774).

copyright was lost upon publication. Thereafter, the author's rights were solely those granted under the Statute of Anne. Thus, the positive law prevailed, but natural law, as embodied in the common law, was also recognized up until the point of publication.

Like much of English law, copyright law immigrated to North America with the English settlers. The framers of the U.S. Constitution were well aware of the *Donaldson* case when they drafted the Copyright Clause. The 1790 Copyright Act, the first U.S. copyright statute, is modeled on the Statute of Anne. Through independent development in other European nations, trade and colonization, international treaties and conventions, copyright law gradually spread around the globe, with significant variations emerging as it was incorporated into different bodies of national law. A number of European countries, for example, developed moral rights jurisprudence granting authors considerably more control than is typical in the countries following the English common law tradition. Eventually, international copyright agreements like the Berne Convention set forth certain common copyright precepts binding on their signatories. More recently, developed nations have used trade agreements to impose this uniquely Western set of laws on countries like China that had no copyright tradition.[5]

The Influence Game

From the very first adoption of a national copyright law, the legislative bodies that make copyright law have been subject to considerable pressure from groups like the Stationers who profit most from publishing monopolies. As different copyright industries became economically and politically powerful, they successfully lobbied legislators to expand the scope and duration of copyright protections. Copyright now provides protection for literary, dramatic, choreographic, pictorial, graphic, sculptural, architectural, musical and audiovisual works, and sound recordings. Those categories include most conceivably expressive works and some surprising ones, such as software. Copyright's original duration has undergone a succession of expansions from its original maximum of 28 years to the current life of the author plus 70 years, with special provisions for corporate or pseudonymous authors, all of which easily push the period for protection beyond a century. With each expansion for new copyrights, the terms of pre-existing copyrights have also been lengthened, keeping works out of the public domain far longer than the Founders anticipated.[6]

---

5 *See* WILLIAM P. ALFORD, TO STEAL A BOOK IS AN ELEGANT OFFENSE 4–5 (1995).

6 17 U.S.C. §§ 302–304 (2006). The Berne Convention sets a minimum duration of life of the author plus 50 years, but a number of countries including the U.S. have ratcheted protections even higher.

Invaluable work by Jessica Litman documented the enormous influence the copyright industries exert on the formation of copyright law in the United States. In 1909, at the time of the first major revision of the Copyright Act, the Register of Copyrights and Congressional leaders essentially threw up their hands in dismay at the prospect of legislators negotiating revision of an act that had already become hopelessly complicated and arcane, the exclusive province of narrowly specialized lawyers and the industries they served. Congress adopted the practice of inviting influential copyright industries to negotiate out the provisions of copyright revisions, a practice it has since adhered to whenever the existing regime needs significant modifications to adapt to changing circumstances. The lobbyists from the major industries hash out language they think they can live with and the legislative machinery grinds out a new or revised copyright provision. In short, copyright lobbyists often do more than merely influence American copyright law—they may, in some instances, actually draft it. Once the representatives of the major industries have reached agreement, Congress gives their work the legislative imprimatur, doubtless grateful to have been spared the necessity of actually reading the often impenetrable, if not incomprehensible, provisions of the bill.[7]

Since copyright law creates rights for private parties, it is perhaps not surprising that it attracts significant lobbying, but the abdication of drafting to the interested parties surely deviates from best legislative practices. While I focus here on the history of U.S. copyright law, since I know it best, copyright legislation in other countries is quite evidently subject to similar influence. During the consideration of the United Kingdom's Digital Economy Bill in 2010, for example, news got out that a proposed amendment to the bill was actually drafted by recording industry lobbyists and entered on their behalf by members of the House of Lords.[8]

A process that allows industries to negotiate out the content of the laws has obvious flaws. First and foremost, not all interested parties are likely to be represented in the negotiations. Not all authors belong to associations that can be said to represent their interests: thus painters, sculptors, choreographers, theatrical directors, and computer programmers were unrepresented in the conferences preceding the 1976 copyright revision that produced the current Copyright Act. New, nascent, or as-yet-unthought-of industries that impact copyrights are unrepresented. Astoundingly, the sound recording industry was not a player in the

---

7 *See* Jessica Litman, Digital Copyright 35–63 (2001).

8 Cory Doctorow, *Leaked Documents: UK Record Industry Wrote Web-Censorship Amendment*, Boing Boing (Mar. 11, 2010, 8:00 AM), http://boingboing.net/2010/03/11/leaked-documents-uk.html.

20-year negotiations leading up to the same revision, because sound recordings were not granted copyright protection until 1972. While some lobbying groups, such as library associations, may claim to represent some aspects of the public interest, the public itself has, historically, been excluded. Instead, entrenched copyright industries have dominated the negotiations, though their interests have often been at odds with the unrepresented public interest. Not surprisingly, the compromises resulting from negotiations among industries tend to produce enormously complicated laws, difficult for anyone but specialists to understand, that contain very broad protections for the industries and very narrowly drawn exceptions protecting public interests such as educational and fair uses.[9]

Copyright legislation, like legislation generally, presents a collective action problem. In a seminal work, Mancur Olson observed that a small, organized, well-financed minority may override the will of the inchoate majority in a democracy. The minority may "capture" the legislature.[10] Historically, the mass of copyright users was insufficiently organized to effectively assert its own interests as against well-organized, deep-pocketed copyright industries. The playing field began to shift ever so slightly in the mid 1990's as the Internet, for the first time, enabled public interest groups, scholars, and ordinary users to coordinate opposition to copyright industry proposals. Nonetheless, the process that produced the Digital Millennium Copyright Act,[11] arguably the most significant piece of copyright legislation since the 1976 revision, illustrates little change from the historical pattern of copyright legislating.

The DMCA backs up the industries' use of digital rights management (DRM) systems with legal prohibitions against circumventing DRM. The negotiations over the act pitted copyright industries against a loose confederation of technology providers, Internet service providers (ISPs), and public interest representatives like librarians, consumer protection advocates, and academics. The public interest representatives used the Internet to organize vociferous public opposition to many provisions of the act. In the end though, the final provisions of the act followed the traditional pattern: extraordinarily complex provisions establishing broad protections and very narrow exceptions. The copyright industries got their protections. The ISPs got a safe harbor against claims of copyright liability based on the infringing activities of their subscribers. Despite their participation in the process, technology providers and public interest advocates got few concessions,

9 *See*, Litman, *supra* note 7, at 46–63.

10 *See* Mancur Olson, The Logic of Collective Action: Public Goods and the Theory of Groups (1965).

11 17 U.S.C. §§ 512, 1201–1205 (2006).

and users were saddled with severe prohibitions and penalties devoid of broad fair use exceptions.[12]

The influence game is now played on a global scale. If multinational copyright industries fail to achieve their goals by influencing the legislature in one country, they may still achieve them in another. More importantly, they may pursue protections through the back door of international treaty negotiations with minimal interference from pesky public interest advocates. In the increasingly common practice of policy laundering, compliance with international treaties or trade agreements is used to leverage passage of domestic protective legislation that might otherwise fail. Such legislation increasingly takes the form of paracopyright laws like the DMCA and, more recently, so-called "three strikes" rules requiring ISPs to disconnect infringing users.[13]

The DMCA began as a set of recommendations by a Clinton Administration Task Force strongly influenced by the demands of the copyright industries for expanded protections that would make them comfortable taking their content online. The industries argued that without expanded copyright protection and legal prohibitions against circumvention of digital rights management, they would be foolhardy to take their content online where it might readily be appropriated by others. The Task Force produced a White Paper recommending many such protections, including DMCA-like protections.[14] Its recommendations set off a storm of criticism from technology providers and various author and public interest groups, organizing for the first time through the Internet. Consequently, the legislation spawned by the White Paper stalled in Congress. Thereafter, the Administration simply took its proposals to the World Intellectual Property Organization (WIPO) as part of ongoing negotiations over a proposed copyright treaty. While the U.S. did not get the full panoply of protections it requested, the resulting WIPO Copyright Treaty[15] did require signatories to provide legal protection and remedies against technological circumvention. Ultimately, the

---

12 *See* Litman, *supra* note 7, at 126–7.

13 *See* Greg Sandoval, *U.K Embraces 'Three Strikes' for Illegal File Sharing*, CnetNews, Apr. 8, 2010, http://news.cnet.com/8301-31001_3-20002018-261.html.

14 Information Infrastructure Task Force, Intellectual Property And The National Information Infrastructure: The Report Of The Working Group On Intellectual Property Rights (1995).

15 WIPO Copyright Treaty, Art. 11, 12, Dec. 20, 1996, *available at* http://www.wipo.int/treaties/en/ip/wct/trtdocs_wo033.html#P87_12240.

DMCA emerged from the process of treaty implementation by Congress.[16] The U.S. continues to push for DMCA-like provisions in trade negotiations.

An even more efficient form of policy laundering occurs where negotiators bundle intellectual property agreements together with trade agreements. Given the significant contribution of intellectual property products to the gross national product, successive administrations, regardless of party affiliation, have proven quite receptive to industry arguments favoring strong copyright protection, and U.S negotiators have pushed for concessions from trading partners. Thus, those countries that wish to obtain the benefits of membership in the WTO must adhere to the TRIPs agreement mandating that members ensure intellectual property protections. Post-TRIPs, the United States and the EU continued to push for enhanced protection and enforcement through bilateral and regional trade agreements with their trading partners.

During the writing of this book, over a dozen countries, including the U.S., the E.U., and Japan, were in the process of negotiating the Anti-Counterfeiting Trade Agreement (ACTA) outside of the usual international forums for multilateral agreements. ACTA, once negotiated, is likely to impose a higher standard of intellectual property enforcement than that mandated by TRIPs.[17] Developing nations were largely excluded from the highly secretive negotiations. The Obama Administration designated the agreement as an executive agreement, not requiring Congressional approval before becoming effective. The Office of the U.S. Trade Representative initially refused to release official information to the general public about the substance of the negotiations on "national security" grounds, even as unofficial leaks indicated that the draft agreement contained provisions mandating Internet disconnection for repeat copyright infringers, criminalization of peer-to-peer file sharing, and border searches of iPods.[18] Nonetheless, drafts of the agreement *were* made available to over 40 well-connected lobbyists under nondisclosure agreements.[19] In short, copyright industries and their lobbyists now push national governments to negotiate stronger, longer copyright protection not merely domestically, but globally.

---

16 *See* Litman, *supra* note 7, at 129–45.

17 Electronic Frontier Foundation, *Anti-Counterfeiting Trade Agreement*, http://www.eff.org/issues/acta (last visited May 12, 2011.)

18 David Kravets, *Special Interests See 'Classified' Copyright Treaty; You Can't*, Wired (Oct. 14, 2009, 1:27 PM), http://www.wired.com/threatlevel/2009/10/specialinterests-peek-at-copyrighttreaty/.

19 James Love, *White House Shares The ACTA Internet Text With 42 Washington Insiders Under Non Disclosure Agreements*, Knowledge Ecology International (Oct. 13, 2009, 4:10 PM), http://kelonline.org/node/660.

Even as copyright has spread around the world over several centuries, scholars, courts, legislators, and copyright industries have elaborated several after-the-fact theoretical justifications providing different answers to the fundamental question "Why copyright?" The Stationers were the first to turn to philosophy in the form of natural rights arguments to justify copyright entitlements, but they were certainly not the last to bend philosophical argument to the task of serving copyright interests. The philosophical theories establish the rhetorical framework for the debate over the goals and the appropriate scope of copyright protection.

Three Not Entirely Satisfactory Theories

In the absence of a well-developed theory justifying copyright at the time of the Statute of Anne, theorists drew liberally on theories of property, personality rights, and economics to produce justifications for the newly minted regime. Over time, roughly three justificatory frameworks emerged from the theoretical stew, albeit with some overlap, some divergence in naming, and a good bit of fuzziness at the margins: labor theory, personhood, and utilitarianism. The first two presume natural, innate rights of creators. The third is a creature of positive law. All are drawn from theories originally promulgated with respect to physical property, real or personal, and none map perfectly onto the rights in intangible, creative works established by the Statute of Anne and its successors. As philosophies, each suffers from logical inconsistencies and near complete lack of empirical verification.

Labor Theory

Labor theory justifies copyright based on the right of authors to benefit from the labor they invest in their works. John Locke's *Second Treatise of Government*[20] provides the foundation for this justification. Locke reasoned that individuals have, by "natural law," a property right in their bodies and, consequently, in the fruits of the labor produced by their bodies. A farmer who invests labor in land and takes it from a state of nature, where it is part of the common, obtains ownership rights by mixing his labor with the land and thereby increasing its value. There are two qualifications to this principle: there must be "enough and as good" left in common for others and the farmer must not accumulate so much property that some is wasted. Locke's treatise dealt with the ownership of physical property, particularly real property, not with intellectual properties like copyrights. The philosopher was dead and buried before the Statute of Anne was adopted.

---

20 John Locke, Two Treatises of Government, Book II, Ch. V ("Of Property") (c. 1690).

There are a number of problems with labor theory even as applied to land. Why does one have a property right in one's own body? Why would one own the labor of that body, much less real estate cultivated by that labor? Human slavery existed for millennia and persisted in Locke's own lifetime. Locke's bald assertion that these are natural rights reflects a worthy aspiration but not actual human practice in his own time. Even granting the existence of property rights in one's body and labor, why would the ownership right encompass ownership of the land rather than merely ownership of, say, a particular season's crop? Sharecropping arrangements certainly divide the two kinds of ownership. Does the addition of labor necessarily add to the value of land or is that merely the assumption of a man who was a product of an agrarian society? If labor alone justifies property rights, why should those rights pass by inheritance to lazy heirs? Beyond these obvious questions, the "enough and as good" and "waste" provisos run counter to known human behavior as reflected in recorded history.

As a descriptive account of the development of Western property rights, labor theory appears to be entirely counterfactual. Locke rests his labor theory on the assumption of an initial state of nature in which all land was undeveloped and free to common use. As he put it, "Thus in the beginning all the world was America …"[21] (conveniently ignoring millions of Native Americans already occupying the "New" World when Europeans arrived there.) Unoccupied land could be turned into property by labor so long as no one took or wasted too much. History teaches, to the contrary, that for millennia property was acquired by conquest and kept by force of arms—martial might made property rights. In England, ownership by the Crown only gradually devolved during and after the Middle Ages to ownership by private individuals. European acquisition of lands by "discovery" and occupation during the Age of Exploration (the 1400s through 1600s) is more accurately described as the outright appropriation of land by force of arms and genocide.

Notwithstanding the obvious weaknesses of labor theory as regards real property, later proponents of strong protections for intellectual works extended variations of this theory to copyright and other forms of intellectual property. The basic normative argument holds that the labor invested by an author in writing a novel or a play, for example, should entitle her to control the work and receive compensation for its sale. Underlying this argument is the assumption that labor is unpleasant, compared to recreation, and will be avoided unless the laborer receives some benefit from it.[22] Clearly, this straightforward normative reading

---

21 *Id.*

22 *See* Justin Hughes, *The Philosophy of Intellectual Property*, 77 Geo. L.J. 287, 303 (1988).

of labor theory is *not* what the Statute of Anne had in mind. A natural law right based on labor would be a perpetual, complete right, as argued by the Stationers, not a copying monopoly limited to a certain term of years post-publication. If fair compensation is the goal, there is nothing in copyright law that assures the fairness of compensation to the author who invests labor. It is often the publisher who reaps the bulk of the benefits of the author's labor. Nor does this argument address "flash of inspiration" creativity where an idea seems to leap fully formed into its creator's mind, with little or no "labor." Coleridge's poem *Kubla Khan*, for example, came to him in a dream, probably induced by opium.[23] He simply wrote it down on awaking. Would it therefore be less deserving of copyright protection than, say, a Victoria's Secret catalog produced by the labor of photographers, ad writers, and so on? J.K. Rowling's inspiration for the Potter series apparently occurred in a flash of inspiration, though it took her years to elaborate on it. Yet her compensation has certainly exceeded that of other authors who labored equally hard or harder on their own works. What about creators who actually enjoy the process of creation—no pain, no copyright gain? Moreover, no one creates in a vacuum. Every creator draws on the culture of which he or she is a part, building on works by others who went before. The Potter books build on centuries of accumulated stories and legends about wizards and witches, fell creatures, magic, and even English public school life. Labor theory entirely fails to acknowledge the cumulative nature of information and the creativity that both springs from the cultural base and augments it for the benefit of future creators. Nonetheless, the fundamental principle that labor deserves reward has inherent appeal and has exerted a strong influence on the development of copyright law.

Personhood

The "personhood" or "moral rights" approach to copyright also claims innate rights in authors, primarily founded on G.W.F. Hegel's theory of property. While tied to difficult arguments regarding the nature of human will, the gist of the theory is that in order to achieve personal self-actualization an individual must control resources in his environment. Certain objects are so closely integrated with personality, so essential to individual human freedom, that they become the individual's property.[24] The individual's personality is manifested by his occupation of or identification with the property. Thus, the Potter books become Rowling's property because they express her personality.

---

23 Nancy C. Andreasen, The Creative Brain: the Science of Genius 19–22 (2005).

24 *See* Hughes, *supra* note 22, at 331–9.

Like labor theory, the personhood justification was originally propounded in the context of physical property, but later scholars adapted it to intangible, intellectual property. And, like labor theory, personhood has certain conceptual issues. Obviously, there must be some limitations granting property rights based on such self-identification: distinctions must be made between property that is truly "personal" and that which is fungible, between valid and invalid "identifications."[25] How does one identify a personality interest? How much personality much be invested in a work to qualify it for protection? What about works like databases or maps or software, or any kind of collective work, that do not seem particularly rooted in personality—no protection for them? If a work is essential to one's personality, how can one then sell it for hard cash?[26] But, like labor theory, personhood contains a kernel argument with inherent appeal: that at least some creative works express the personality of their creator and the link between the creator and her work deserves protection.

In copyright, personhood finds its strongest expression in the moral rights laws of France, Germany, and a number of other European countries. Such laws confer on authors the rights to prevent mutilation or destruction of their works, to assure proper attribution, and to receive royalties from serial sales and rentals of the work. These moral rights are equally as important as the alienable rights of economic exploitation, including rights of reproduction, distribution, adaptation, public performance and display, or the "neighboring rights" granted to performers, recording studios, and broadcasters. Personhood theory bears little relationship to the very practical framework established by the Statute of Anne. Rights based entirely on personhood would presumably be inalienable (as moral rights are in civil law countries) and more complete than the limited right established under the Statute. They should presumably last at least for the author's lifetime, which they did not under many early copyright statutes, though they well exceed that limitation now. Even those countries following the moral rights tradition set limits of scope and duration on the economic exploitation rights associated with copyrights.

Utilitarianism

Personhood considerations had relatively little influence on the development of copyright law in common law countries like the United Kingdom and its former colonies, including the United States, Canada, India, and Australia. Instead, an instrumental interpretation of Locke's writings dominated copyright discourse in common law countries and strongly affected it even in civil law countries. Lest

25 *Id.*

26 *Id.*, at 339–50.

his bald assertion that labor deserves reward proved unconvincing, Locke offered a supplemental argument: granting people property rights in the results of their labor increases the collective wealth of society.[27] Translated into copyright terms, this utilitarian (or economic or market) justification for copyright suggests that it is necessary to give authors incentives, in the form of limited monopoly rights, in order to encourage them to create works that will ultimately benefit the public. The guarantee of reward to the creator is not payment for labor invested, but for the societal benefit received from the work. Common law countries focus on the economic rights of the owner of the copyright, whether that owner is the original author or an assignee like a publisher or a movie studio.

Utilitarians use positive copyright law as an instrument to encourage the creation and dissemination of works to the public. The language of the Statute of Anne was strongly utilitarian though it was drafted before the full flowering of utilitarianism as a philosophy later in the century. It was entitled "An Act for the Encouragement of Learning, by vesting the Copies of Printed Books in the Authors or purchasers of such Copies, during the Times therein mentioned."[28] The primary goal is encouragement of learning; the instrumentality is the copyright. The U.S. Copyright and Patent Clause, similarly, empowers Congress "To promote the Progress of Science and useful Arts, by securing for limited Times to Authors and Inventors the exclusive Right to their Respective Writings and Discoveries."[29] The primary goal is to promote the progress of science and useful arts; the limited monopoly is the means to that end. Happily, copyright may also reward the author for her labor, though to a degree determined by the market and limited in duration. We know from constitutional text and history, and later judicial interpretation, that the framers of the American Constitution intentionally created a utilitarian provision, not a statutory recognition of a perpetual innate right. With their contemporaries in England, they were quite distrustful of monopolies and intended to keep such entitlements within strict limits.[30] Locke himself, living under the Stationers' monopoly, suggested that public domain books should be open for anyone to print and that even new books should be printable by any publisher after a certain term of years. Even the first French copyright laws, for

[27] *Id.*, at 299.

[28] Statute of Anne, 1710, 8 Ann., c.19 (Eng.).

[29] U.S. Const., Art. I, § 8, cl. 8.

[30] *See* Patterson and Birch, *supra* note 2, at 256–8.

all their concern with moral rights, contained a fair dose of utilitarian concern for the public good.[31]

The key assumptions of the utilitarian view are economic. In a market economy, creators will not invest time and resources to produce works unless they are assured of a reasonable return on their investment. If published works could be freely copied, authors would be unable to get such a return and, consequently, would refuse to produce works that might benefit the public at large. Copyright laws creating limited monopolies will incentivize the production of creative works. Society as a whole will ultimately benefit from the dissemination of works that educate, entertain, promote innovation, and, eventually, enter the public domain where they will be free for all to enjoy and for future creators to build upon. These assumptions are based, at least in part, on the underlying Lockean assumption that labor is painful and people will avoid it unless they receive some reward. The utilitarian approach lends itself to economic analyses that often focus on the peculiar "public goods" characteristics of informational works that distinguish them from other forms of property.

In general, public goods are goods, like national defense, that markets will not supply on their own initiative and the absence of which results in harm to the public. Two characteristics distinguish public goods from private property: nonrivalrous consumption and nonexcludability. Nonrivalrous goods can be used by any number of people without being used up, and use by one person does not preclude use by another. In the case of informational works, any number of people can enjoy the same movie, or novel, or song, or do research in the same nonfictional work without putting the slightest dent in the availability of the works for others to enjoy. Informational works are also nonexcludable because the only way to profit from an informational work is to release it for public consumption, and once the work is released, it is very difficult to exclude nonpaying users.

In the analog world, once a novel was published, any competitor with a printing press could copy the book at considerably lower cost than the costs incurred by the author's publisher, which would have to pay the author, invest in editing, marketing, and so on, as well as pay for the costs of printing. Consequently, the unauthorized competitor could sell the book at a lower price, destroying the author's market. This problem is accentuated by digital technologies. Once a digital version of a copyrighted work is released, even consumers may easily make unauthorized copies and distribute them. Consequently, it may be difficult for the

---

[31] *See* James Boyle, The Public Domain: Enclosing the Commons of the Mind 28–33 (2008).

creator of an informational work to receive a fair return on its investment and, absent such return, many creators might refuse to invest in informational works at all. The close secrecy in which the Potter manuscripts and printed books were held prior to the official release date, as well as the bootleg copies of the movies that rapidly appeared on the Internet, bear witness to the difficulties associated with public goods.

Copyright law attempts to solve the public goods problem by imposing a monopoly in order to insure a fair return to creators, but limiting the monopoly in order to assure public access to the protected works. In other words, the copyright solution represents a trade-off between the interests of creators and the public. Utilitarians generally focus on the proper balance between incentives and public access. Law and economics scholars typically approach this problem as a basic cost–benefit analysis. The goal is to tailor copyright laws to provide the minimum incentives necessary to induce creation without unduly restricting the rights of the public, and future creators, to use the work.

In the U.S., courts interpreting copyright statutes have created a number of corollary doctrines in attempts to fine-tune the balance between incentives and access. The idea/expression dichotomy, for example, excludes ideas and facts from copyright protection and firmly places them in the public domain open to use by all. The fair use doctrine establishes a set of rules by which copyrighted works can be used for certain publicly beneficial ends, such as educational uses, without permission from the copyright holder. With the advent of digitization and global networks, the proper location of the balance point between creator incentives and public access has inspired considerable debate as each new digital technology requires recalibration of the competing interests.

As with labor theory and personhood, there are some holes in the basic utilitarian argument. It is often difficult to define or quantify the societal benefit being sought. Economic analyses, in particular, focus on monetary costs and benefits to the exclusion of nonmonetizable goals like public education, dissemination of information, and innovation that are clearly fundamental to the copyright regime as originally envisioned. They tend to focus on producer interests to the exclusion of the interests of users and future creators. Even if we could define societal benefit, copyright compensation is not in any way aligned with the degree of societal benefit. If anything, the largest monetary rewards often seem to compensate the least "worthy" works. In fact, copyright protection is granted even if the work is never published and societal benefit is zero.

The connection between incentives and creation is tenuous at best. For thousands of years, from the earliest known civilizations up through the Renaissance and the beginning of the Enlightenment in the West, creative works were produced and distributed without benefit of copyright. In non-Western countries like China that developed no copyright tradition, creative works nonetheless appeared. Creators may produce works for any number of noneconomic reasons such as a desire for fame, a psychological compulsion to create, or as an expression of religious faith. In the digital environment, users have individually and collectively produced a wide variety of creative and informational works, from fan fiction to comprehensive encyclopedias, often for no economic remuneration at all. No incentives are needed for such creators, though they may be needed for others.

Publishers certainly require a return on their investment, and the development of copyright was a natural adjunct of the development of market economies in which for-profit businesses, rather than wealthy patrons, became the primary supporters of artists and the distributors of their works. Today, publishers' formerly dominant position in the copyright hierarchy is increasingly challenged by the digitization and decentralization of information production and distribution. As the costs of copying and distribution approach zero, the need for incentives to publishers correspondingly diminishes. The appropriate balance between creator incentives and public access thus presents a moving target whose location seems to be subject to the copyright equivalent of Heisenberg's uncertainty principle: the more the observer focuses on one of the paired goals of copyright, the less he is likely to get a fix on the other.

Problems with the Theories

As the reader may have noticed, the three theories of copyright do not require precision. None offers, nor requires, correlation to real copyright industries operating in complex interconnection with technological, social, economic, or political systems. They are, as philosophical positions are prone to be, quite abstract in nature. They propound very general principles that recognize few significant differences between, for example, copyright industries that produce books and those that produce movies or video games. None is entirely satisfactory standing alone—each presents its own logical inconsistencies. None has supplanted the others—as yet there is no unified theory of copyright. Rather all three persist in various combinations both in legislation and case law.

American courts, while generally adhering to utilitarian principles, have freely used the other theories to bolster their conclusions. For example, in *Mazer v. Stein*,[32] granting copyright protection to the design of a statuary lamp base, the Supreme Court employs both utilitarian and labor reasoning within the same paragraph:

[32] 347 U.S. 201 (1954).

> The economic philosophy behind the clause empowering Congress to grant patents and copyrights is the conviction that encouragement of individual effort by personal gain is the best way to advance public welfare through the talents of authors and inventors. … Sacrificial days devoted to such creative activities deserve rewards commensurate with the services rendered.[33]

In *Bleistein v. Donaldson Lithographing Co.*,[34] granting protection to circus advertisements, Justice Holmes observes, in an obvious nod to personhood:

> … a very modest grade of art has in it something irreducible, which is one man's alone. … Personality always contains something unique. It expresses its singularity even in handwriting … [35]

Thus, the courts can pick and choose justifications to suit their leanings in a particular case. The availability of alternative theories may have provided courts with a useful flexibility, but has seldom produced consistency in the law.

Inconsistencies also exist internationally as different countries have emphasized different theories and incorporated them into the substance of their copyright laws, with the most notable split involving the divergent treatment of authorship and moral rights in civil and common law nations. Despite treaties like the Berne Convention and TRIPs promoting harmonization of copyright protections across borders, there remain transnational variations in judicial interpretations of concepts as basic as "originality" with moral rights countries imposing a rather more rigorous standard than common law countries. Variable justifications for copyright produced variable interpretations of its requirements and scope. Thus, some works, such as perfumes, fashion designs, and data compilations receive protection in some countries but not others.[36] Since these variations were integral to the evolutionary path of copyright in each country, they have proven difficult to dislodge notwithstanding the push for harmonization.[37]

The persistence of several competing theories, generally unembarrassed by any proven connection to copyright realities, has provided useful rhetorical tools for industry lobbyists. Both national legislation and international treaties bear the strong imprint of copyright industries employing copyright theories as weapons in their perpetual quest to persuade governments to expand copyright protections.

---

33 *Id.*, at 219.

34 188 U.S. 239 (1903).

35 *Id.*, at 250.

36 Mary LaFrance, Global Issues in Copyright Law 5–38 (2009).

37 *See* Ulla-Maija Mylly, *Harmonizing Copyright Rules for Computer Program Interface Protection*, article draft, 2–3, in the author's possession.

If one theory does not support a desired outcome, perhaps another theory can be employed. If, for example, Congress is not sufficiently moved by the prospects of lost profits, a copyright industry may rail against the injustice of free riders reaping where they have not sown. The very abstractness and generality of the justificatory theories makes them particularly amenable to use as propaganda. With the popularization of digital media and the Internet, the debate over the proper scope of copyright protection has become increasingly polarized. It frequently takes the form of a perceived conflict between private property and the commons that grows naturally out of the analogies copyright theorists have drawn between physical property and the creative and informational works protected by copyright law.

Private Property versus the Commons

The three theoretical justifications offered for copyright rely on arguments derived by analogy from earlier theories formulated for tangible, not intangible, property. Participants in the debate over the appropriate scope and duration of copyright protection frequently compare intellectual properties, like copyrights, to real property. Thus, copyright owners claim that their use of digital rights management technologies is comparable to the rightful exclusionary act of a landowner building a fence around his property. Comparing copyright ownership to ownership of land or chattels, they denounce infringers as thieves and pirates. Proponents of more limited copyright entitlements compare the expansion of intellectual property rights to the English land enclosure movement, characterizing it as an unjustifiable land grab from the commons formerly available for public use.[38] They use the rhetoric of public access, communal creativity, and free exchange of information. The debate over copyright protection is subsumed in the larger debate over intellectual property protection for informational works in general. Even use of the term "intellectual property" is contested on grounds that it carries too many implications of "propertyness" for rights like copyrights and patents which are actually structured as limited monopolies, not perpetual ownership rights.

The two sides frame the debate over control of information as a conflict between private property and the commons. "Private property" generally refers to exclusive ownership by individuals or corporate entities. Interpretations of the "commons" vary: some commentators use the term to describe completely open access to informational works, while others equate the commons with the public

38 *See* Boyle, *supra* note 31, at 37.

domain, which itself has multiple definitional variations.[39] Scholars wrestle with tragedies and comedies of the commons, not to mention "anticommons," in which too many property rights defeat innovation, and "semicommons," which mix elements of private and public property.

Garrett Hardin popularized the phrase "tragedy of the commons" in a work concerned not with intellectual property but with natural resources and population control. He posited that resources owned in common are inevitably subject to overexploitation, creating a tragedy of the commons.[40] Hardin and others suggested that the only solutions to that tragedy in the tangible world were either centralized government control or private property ownership,[41] thereby initiating a discourse that recognized only polar opposites. Property scholars have pointed out that this binary discourse entirely fails to recognize that some resources, like public roads, are actually most successful when "owned" by the state, producing "comedies" of the commons.[42] The rapid economic development of China in recent years, under a system that mixes central control with aspects of private ownership, should put paid to the notion that an either/or choice is the only available option. Thus, the discourse has flaws even as applied to the tangible world. The binary approach is yet more suspect when applied to public goods like copyrights. Informational commons are not subject to overexploitation, because informational works are consumed nonrivalrously. With respect to such works, the tragedy of the commons, if it exists, results instead in reduced incentives for creation or distribution.

High protectionists, who advocate strong copyright protection, predict just such a tragedy of the commons if informational works are too readily appropriated. Importing Hardin's argument about natural resources into the world of informational resources, they advocate private property–like rights as the solution for this tragedy. Not surprisingly, major copyright industries gravitate toward high protection, private property models, employing arguments grounded in the utilitarian necessity for preserving economic incentives as well as labor-based fairness arguments favoring producers over "freeriding" pirates. Low protectionists point out that, unlike real property, intellectual properties must

---

[39] *See* Pamela Samuelson, *Enriching Discourse on Public Domains*, 55 Duke L.J. 783, 786–813 (2006).

[40] *See* Garrett Hardin, *The Tragedy of the Commons*, 162 Science. 1243, 1243–8 (1968).

[41] *See* Elinor Ostrom, Governing the Commons: The Evolution of Institutions for Collective Action 8–14 (1990).

[42] *See* Carol M. Rose, *The Comedy of the Commons: Custom, Commerce, and Inherently Public Property*, 53 U. Chi. L. Rev. 711, 723 (1986).

build on prior works. Overprotection of essential intellectual building blocks may impoverish the public domain causing underutilization of intellectual resources, the "tragedy of the anticommons."[43] Strong monopolies, they argue, also impose real costs in the form of lost public access to culture.

The parties to this discourse agree that legal regimes must achieve some balance between incentives and public access, but each camp would strike the balance at different locations on the spectrum between strong and weak protection. Copyright owners and users tend to devolve to the extremes. Owners demand compensation for all potential uses of their works, a scope of protection never previously granted by copyright. Some of them employ digital rights management technology to control access to their works. Users demand and, with the help of technology sometimes achieve, almost unlimited free access. Technology and Internet service providers have come to occupy a somewhat uncomfortable position between the two poles as they seek to assure maximum usage of their own goods and services without incurring liability for their users' infringements.

Both the pro-commons and pro-property arguments have known limitations. Pro-commons formulations ignore distributional inequities in the exploitation of intellectual commons that disadvantage developing nations and indigenous populations.[44] Pro-property formulations slight the importance of shared culture, innovation, and communal creativity.[45] Moreover, those debating the scope of copyright protection presume, without proof, that the setting of legal entitlements bears a linear cause–effect relationship to production and distribution of works. Ownership forms are simply presumed to be determinative of good husbandry of the resource. Both approaches fail to recognize the necessary synergy between copyright ownership, which protects the interests of current creators, and the public domain that provides the materials for future creators and ensures dissemination to the public.[46]

Reasoning by analogy is a time-honored and useful tool. However, the reasoning can only be as convincing as the analogy is apt. Arguments by analogy assume

43 *See,* Michael A. Heller, *The Tragedy of the Anticommons: Property in the Transition from Marx to Markets*, 111 Harv. L. Rev. 621–22 (1998).

44 *See* Anupam Chander & Madhavi Sunder, *The Romance of the Public Domain*, 92 Cal. L. Rev. 1331,

1334–5 (2004).

45 *See* Carol M. Rose, *The Several Futures of Property: Of Cyberspace and Folk Tales, Emission Trades and Ecosystems*, 83 Minn. L. Rev. 129, 140–6 (1998).

46 *See* Carol M. Rose, *Romans, Roads, And Romantic Creators: Traditions Of Public Property in the Information Age,* 66 Law & Contemp. Probs. 89, 101–2 (2003).

that if some aspects of A are like B, other aspects of A are like B—an assumption that is sometimes problematic. For example, the early common law practice of reasoning by analogy from the rule of capture for wild animals, established in cases like *Pierson v. Post*,[47] to "fugitive" resources like oil and gas had disastrous consequences for resource conservation. Legal rules granting ownership to the first to take possession of such resources encouraged overexploitation and discouraged resource management. Today, the oil and gas industries are invariably regulated by laws formulated to deal with specific conditions of those industries—which proved to be not at all similar to conditions for hunting foxes. As the public goods argument makes clear, reasoning by analogy from tangible property to works of the mind carries similar risks, particularly where such reasoning lacks empirical verification.

Failure to Test the Theories

In point of fact, until quite recently, empirical research designed to establish a factual basis for any of the copyright theories has been limited and sporadic. Scientists view a "theory" as a model of reality whose validity must be empirically proven if it is to stand. Theories generate testable hypotheses about causal relationships that produce certain phenomena. If empirical evidence supports the hypotheses, the theory is accepted, always subject to further proof or disproof, as a valid explanation for the phenomenon.[48] Evolution is a "theory" not in the sense that it remains an unproven hypothesis, but in the sense that overwhelming empirical evidence, gathered over 150 years, shows that evolution has, and does, occur. Most copyright scholars, to the contrary, have approached the various copyright theories as philosophical "theory," existing in the realm of ideas and unverifiable by empirical testing. If Darwin had behaved like a legal philosopher rather than a scientist, he would have simply outlined the theory of evolution, based on little more than his own speculations about how the world must work, then opened the floor to a debate in which basic precepts could be offered, even considered to be established, without empirical testing. In copyright law, we have trusted to the legal philosophers for 300 years. One theory or another has been favored in particular nations or on particular legal issues, but there have been only rare attempts to establish that any of them work as advertised in the real world of creators, distributors, and users of copyrighted works.

---

[47] 3 Cai. R. 175, 2 Am. Dec. 264 (N.Y. Sup. Ct. 1805).

[48] *See* Robert M. Lawless, Jennifer K. Robbennolt, and Thomas S. Ulen, Empirical Methods in Law 8–9 (2010).

Labor theory and personhood proceed from essentially moralistic assumptions: an inherent right of ownership in the body, an innate drive to express personality through possession. Those bare assertions can, to some extent, be directly challenged by modern biology, psychology, neuroscience, and related fields. At a minimum, their claimed relationships to copyright law could be tested. Recent research suggests that *homo sapiens* is a uniquely social species for which sharing and mimicry are tools for learning and building culture. History establishes that many non-Western cultures function quite successfully without private property. How do these facts accord with theories that labor justifies ownership or that individuality must be expressed through possessions? Utilitarian theory fairly begs for empirical verification: it assumes a linear relationship between copyright incentives and creative production that should be testable. Yet, for reasons explored in the next chapter, there has been little systematic study by the legal academy of the effects of copyrights on the industries they are alleged to encourage.

To date, there is little empirical evidence to support even the basic correlation between copyright incentives and creativity, progress of the arts and sciences, or improved public access. The empirical studies we do have tend to focus on markets. We lack comprehensive analyses of copyright systems, as systems, that include the full panoply of social, cultural, and political, as well as economic, issues. This leaves us, by and large, stuck with three philosophical positions, none of which were designed with copyright in mind and which bend only grudgingly to accommodate the special circumstances of creative works. We are locked into an unproductive, binary debate between high and low protection that pays little heed to the concrete realities of copyright systems.

The persistence of three competing theories, and the lack of verification of any of them, leaves the field wide open for powerful lobbyists to exert influence over copyright legislation. In the absence of proven damage to the communal cultural enterprise, the rhetoric of property and the realities of economic and political power tend to favor established copyright industries over nascent industries and over the public interest in access. Those who wish to find a middle ground may resort to contract, in the form of open source or creative commons licenses, but need not hope to find it in copyright law as it is currently constructed. Moreover, the reliance on analogies to real property incorporates a central failing of real property law that we have only begun to understand in recent decades—the failure to consider to see each parcel of real estate as situated within a larger ecosystem. However, the emerging analogy of information to natural ecosystems offers some hope that a more nuanced approach can be crafted and invites analysis within a complexity framework.

Information as an Ecosystem

Some scholars have suggested an alternative view of copyright as part of an information ecosystem in which a complementary, rather than an oppositional, relationship, exists between intellectual property rights and the public domain.[49] Some suggest that intellectual property should be viewed as a "semi-commons" in which private and common uses are dynamically related.[50] They reject the analogy to real property and offer a different analogy, to natural ecosystems, as a more appropriate framework for analysis. Their work suggests that if we are going to approach copyright through reasoning by analogy, we should exercise more care in choosing the analogy. This line of reasoning opens up the possibility of a less polarizing approach to the debate between private property and the commons.

Some of these scholars cite empirical studies of alternative ownership models, such as common-pool resources or "limited common" property, in which certain resources are managed in common by a limited group of people which nonetheless has exclusive rights as against all those outside the group. They document situations in which groups such as fishing collectives or irrigation communities successfully own and manage natural resources in common and can exclude others from use of the property.[51] Such work suggests that there may be many workable models of ownership along a spectrum between the extremes of the carefully tended field and the open frontier. It further suggests that important social policies ought not to be based on metaphors, or abstract philosophies, without empirical study to verify their relevance. The information ecosystem approach is clearly congenial to analysis based on complexity theory and science.

To examine the suitability of the ecosystem as analogy, we can look again to the real historical example of the prairies. These ecosystems sustained millions of buffalo, and the Native American tribes dependent on them, without imposition of any formal system of property ownership, for thousands of years. Native Americans saw themselves as an integral part of these ecosystems, existing in a dynamic, complementary relationship with their environment. Private property ownership, in the Western sense, was largely unknown to indigenous peoples. European settlers, on the other hand, brought with them concepts of private

---

49 *See, e.g.,* James Boyle, *A Politics for Intellectual Property: Environmentalism for the Net*, 47 Duke L.J. 87, 108–13 (1997); Peter K. Yu, *Intellectual Property and the Information Ecosystem*, 2005 Mich. St. L. Rev. 1, 6–8 (2005).

50 *See, e.g.,* Robert A. Heverley, *The Information Semi-commons*, 18 Berkeley Tech. L.J. 1127, 1161–83 (2003).

51 *See e.g.*, Ostrom, *supra* note 41.

property and a longstanding perception of nature as an enemy that must be fought and domesticated. They took at face value the biblical injunction to "Be fruitful and multiply; fill the earth and subdue it; have dominion over the fish of the sea, over the birds of the air, and over every living thing that moves on the earth."[52] As a consequence, they slaughtered the prairies' human and animal inhabitants and parceled out the plains. They converted the prairies from grazing land to farmland, employing methods of husbandry that typified the biblical approach to natural resources until the Dust Bowl taught the painful lesson that even the richest land requires careful management to remain productive.

Well before the days of the Dust Bowl, farming proved disastrous in certain tallgrass prairie regions of Kansas and Oklahoma where the soil was too rocky and shallow to sustain cultivation. In those regions, the land was eventually returned to its natural use—grazing—by ranchers who came to understand the interdependence between grasses, herds of bovines, and natural fires. Ranchers now mimic with cattle the migratory patterns of the bison herds and, like the Native Americans before them, use controlled fires to achieve the beneficial ecosystem effects caused by natural fires.[53] The ranchers and farmers learned to manage the prairie within a private property regime; the Native Americans successfully managed it within a non-property regime. Sustainable use of the prairie depended not merely on the particular legal rights granted by the law, but on users' respect for the requirements of each ecosystem. Laws do matter, though they are not all that matters. The legal rights granted to settlers on the prairies contributed to the destruction of most prairie ecosystems, but the settlers' failure to grasp the requirements of the ecosystems also played a role.

The ecosystem analogy suggests that, like different prairie ecosystems, different copyright systems may require different methods of husbandry. With respect to laws regarding ownership, there must be more choices available than the binary choice between private property and the commons. How should we identify a broader range of choices? We might start by establishing the needs of the systems, rather than by imposing a top-down regime based on unverified philosophical assumptions about the systems' responses to legal intervention. We need to push the legal philosophers out of the bar and onto the prairie. We ought to push past analogy and metaphor, past the use of philosophical theories never to be tested, toward the use of theories, in the scientific rather than the philosophical sense,

---

52 *Genesis* 1:28.

53 Aimee Larrabee and John Altman, Last Stand of the Tallgrass Prairie 24, 99–104 (2001).

that are tested against copyright realities. Complexity science offers a more useful framework for this endeavor than antiquated theories derived from philosophies of real property.

We should take as our hypothesis that copyright systems are not merely "like" ecosystems; they are the same kind of systems as a matter of taxonomy. Our efforts should be bent toward mapping out the comprehensive ecology of copyright as biologists would map out the relationships and dependencies in a prairie or as complexity economists map out the relationships in market systems. We ought to explore the many, varied subsystems of copyright to determine what they have in common, how they differ, and what is required to sustain creative productivity in the informational fields regulated by copyright law. Theories guide that exploration but must be tested empirically, not merely offered up as rhetorical flourishes in an unending debate.

To the extent that the existing justifications for copyright are subject to empirical testing, research may validate or disprove them in whole or in part. A complexity framework is likely to provide a more nuanced approach to laws governing creative endeavors than any of the prior theories. On the one hand, it requires actual study of the ways in which individual copyright systems function; on the other, it demands recognition of the broader context, the political, social, economic, and technological landscape, within which the systems operate. A complexity-based approach may even return copyright to its pragmatic roots. Such an approach will, at a minimum, align copyright researchers with those in a variety of other disciplines who use complexity precepts to explore subjects ranging from human history, social behaviors, and cognitive development to planetary ecologies and their sustainability. The next two chapters sketch out the methodologies and goals for such a venture.

Chapter 3
Systems Analysis for the Copyright Ecosystem

It would seem to be self-evident that we must understand how copyright systems work if we wish to draft useful legal rules to govern them. The old justifications for copyright should be tested against the facts; new approaches should be tried and, likewise, tested. Yet relatively few legal scholars pursued empirical studies of copyright until quite recently. This chapter tackles several related issues: the reason that so little empirical work was done in the past; the changes in circumstances that make such work both possible and desirable, and the form or forms an empirically-based systems approach to copyright might take. Initially, it considers definitional questions such as the meaning of terms like "analysis" and "empirical" in the context of complex adaptive systems.

Use of the word "analysis" with regard to study of complex adaptive systems may seem paradoxical in light of the derivation of the word from the Greek for breaking up a whole into its component parts for purposes of study.[1] Complexity theory requires a holistic approach that emphasizes connections and interdependencies whereas "analysis" describes a reductive enterprise, the disconnection of subjects into digestible parts. The reductive approach served science well for centuries but fails utterly to capture the essential nature of complex adaptive systems. In common usage, however, the term "analysis" means studying the interrelationships among component parts, as well as the parts themselves. Systems analysts in computational fields often break down computerized systems to evaluate their component modules, but they also look at the operation of the whole system as well as its parts. Similarly, modern studies of biological systems use a process that involves reduction of complex systems into constituent parts and processes for study, followed by synthesis of those elements to explain the emergent properties of the complex system as a whole.[2] It is in this broader sense that "systems analysis" can apply to complex adaptive systems. Comprehensive understanding of such systems requires empirical observation of their workings.

---

1 Merriam Webster's Collegiate Dictionary, 10th Ed., 41 (1997).

2 Open Book, *Stinging the Dinosaurs*, Harvard Magazine, Nov.–Dec. 2008, at 26.

The word "empirical," as used herein, includes any form of study that methodically gathers and analyzes observable data about copyright systems as they developed or currently operate in the real world. Such techniques include, but are not limited to, techniques that involve quantification or statistical analysis, such as standard economic analyses. Empirical research also includes qualitative studies that probe the reasons for certain behaviors, such as, for example, the motivations that drive creators. Historical or comparative analyses are equally "empirical" in the broad sense. So are descriptive studies that map the flows within a system, such as inputs and outputs, production processes, or networks for production and distribution of creative works, whether or not such flows can be precisely quantified.

Obviously, scholars could apply empirical techniques within a variety of theoretical frameworks, including those of the current philosophical theories justifying copyright with all of their known limitations. Application within a complexity framework, however, offers opportunities to verify whether, in fact, particular copyright systems are complex adaptive systems, and then to develop a more comprehensive understanding of those systems. Within that framework, which is far more adaptable than the static philosophies of the past, researchers can model copyright-related systems and use a variety of empirical techniques to test those models. The time is ripe, if not overdue, for such work.

Past and Present Conditions for Empirical Research

Prior to the turn of the millennium, there were a few efforts to apply empirical techniques to the study of particular aspects of copyright. As might be expected, some law and economics scholars attempted analyses of copyright from the economic standpoint. Notably, Supreme Court Justice Stephen Breyer, then Professor Breyer, took an early look at the economics of book publishing more than 40 years ago in his article *The Uneasy Case for Copyright*.[3] He studied the industry, talked to publishers, analyzed industry surveys, census data, and Copyright Office records, and crunched the real numbers available to him at the time. He concluded: "the case for copyright in books rests not upon proven need, but rather upon uncertainty as to what would happen if protection were removed."[4] He extrapolated from his findings to several proposals then being considered

3 *See* Stephen Breyer, *The Uneasy Case for Copyright: A Study of Copyright in Books, Photocopies, and Computer Programs*, 84 Harv. L. Rev. 281 (1970).

4 *Id.*, at 322.

as part of the revision process that produced the current Copyright Act. Breyer recommended against longer copyright durations and expansion of copyright to cover the new subject matter of computer software. Noting that copyright protection was, at best, a mixed blessing, he observed that the desirability of copyright protection varies from one type of work to another, and one should know the facts about each particular industry before weighing the costs and benefits associated with copyright protection.[5]

His article was, and continues to be, widely cited for its conclusion, but its data-gathering methodology was only rarely emulated in the following decades. Over that period, economic studies were more apt to supply economic theory than real data. The sparseness of detailed empirical work may be attributed to the convergence of several factors, some practical and some attitudinal. On the practical side, real world data, particularly about the workings of the copyright industries, was difficult to collect for most of copyright's history. Even if it could have been collected, the tools for manipulating and analyzing the data were limited. On the attitudinal side, the nature of legal analysis itself and the legal academy's love affair with theoretical inquiry to the exclusion of descriptive work channeled scholars away from empirical studies.

Before the advent of the personal computer and the Internet, the copyright industries controlled much of the data about their own workings that might have been used to estimate the impact of copyright law on them. Such data could be hard to collect because it was not maintained in readily accessible formats or was closely held for reasons of competitive advantage or political strategy. Breyer himself complained about the limited information available to him and admitted that he was forced to do considerable speculation to reach his conclusions.[6] As recently as 1996, a scholar challenging the "incentives-access paradigm" still used Breyer's decades-old figures on book publishing for lack of better data.[7] It was not unusual to find law and economics studies that deployed economic models employing complicated formulas without applying them to any data drawn from real industries. For example, when William Landes and Richard Posner, titans of law and economics scholarship, published their 1989 article on the economic analysis of copyright law, they outlined a formal model of the economics of

---

5 *Id.*, at 351.

6 *Id.*, at 322.

7 *See* Glynn S. Lunney, *Reexamining Copyright's Incentives-Access Paradigm*, 49 VAND. L. REV. 483, 606 (1996).

copyright that was chock full of theoretical formulas, but almost entirely lacking in actual data.[8]

In addition to the difficulties of data collection, potential researchers for most of copyright's history lacked tools powerful enough to analyze large quantities of data, find overarching patterns, and locate discrepancies between copyright's theory and its practice. Immersed as we now are in all forms of electronic technologies, it takes conscious effort to recall the sheer physical effort involved in amassing and organizing data prior to the advent of, and amazingly rapid improvement in, the computing capabilities of the personal computer. As recently as the 1980s, computerized research often involved the scheduling of scarce time at odd hours on massive university-owned computers fed with punch cards. Scholars were sometimes required to do their own programming, employing interfaces that were anything but user-friendly.

Even after industries and the academy adopted personal computers, researchers often worked with unwieldy text-based programs, requiring a multitude of special key combinations to operate basic word processing and spreadsheet programs. The World Wide Web did not exist and the Internet was a playground only for the technologically savvy who were familiar with such esoterica as the gopher protocol[9] and usenet newsgroups.[10] Before Google, search engine results were seldom accurate enough to capture either comprehensive results on the targeted subject or results precise enough to avoid extraneous, irrelevant information. Information did not flow with anything approaching the ease and speed we have grown accustomed to in the last decade or so.

After the mid 1990s, the rapid deployment of user-friendly interfaces on personal computers was complemented by development of the supremely user-friendly World Wide Web with its readily accessible pages and hyperlinks. By the turn of the millennium, Google provided an efficient search system, and users could easily locate and share information through a multiplicity of technologies from email to peer-to-peer file sharing. Internet usage by consumers simply exploded, sparking a tremendous expansion in the available commercial and noncommercial

---

8 *See* William M. Landes and Richard A. Posner, *An Economic Analysis of Copyright Law*, 18 J. Legal Studies 325 (1989).

9 The gopher protocol was an early, text-based protocol that allowed searches and retrievals of documents over the Internet. The World Wide Web largely supplanted it, though it retains a small following of users.

10 Usenet is an Internet discussion system organized into topics called newsgroups. It predated the World Wide Web by more than a decade and was a precursor of Internet fora, blogs, mailing lists, and the like. Usenet is still in operation, but is considerably less popular than the Web.

web content. Blogs, online shopping, social networking—many of us now live a substantial portion of our lives online. Data has become ubiquitous, our ability to parse it with high-powered computers impressive. We can perform with a single smart phone many functions that formerly required an array of powerful computers. Consequently, many of the practical barriers to data collection and analysis have been significantly lowered. The global information ecosystem provides access to vast amounts of information that were previously unavailable. Today, we are more likely to suffer from a surfeit of data, than a dearth of it.

The industries themselves are more likely to have organized their data electronically in databases and more likely to have published at least some of it on publicly accessible Web sites. Some problems with data collection may persist, particularly those involving strategic withholding of information by the industries, or for that matter, strategic release of industry-formulated, intentionally biased data. Nonetheless, considerably more data is available than formerly and we have computing power enough to parse it. We have, however, been slow to apply our new electronic tools to test the basic tenets of copyright law. Beyond the practical difficulties there were significant barriers rooted in the nature of legal analysis generally and the professional emphases of the legal academy in particular. The erection of those barriers begins in the first year of law school as future lawyers are taught to "think like lawyers."

Thinking like a lawyer requires focus on the particulars of individual cases, formulation of arguments for one side or the other, and the marshalling of legal authority and evidence supporting those arguments. The lawyer aims to make an argument that will win a favorable, definitive judgment for her client in an adversarial process that has a definite end point, albeit one that may be delayed for years as the judicial process grinds slowly to its conclusion. Objectivity, the search for broader patterns of behavior, the challenging of established assumptions are not part of the standard legal toolkit. This approach often, though not always, carries over into legal scholarship. A law professor working on an article is likely to start with a particular conclusion in mind, then search through the law and the legal literature for support for his argument, downplaying or countering information that pushes in the other direction.

Empirical scholars, on the other hand, create hypotheses and then look for objective, verifiable data that either support or undermine the hypotheses. Any hypothesis stands or falls based on that data. Empiricists challenge assumptions. They look for patterns in aggregated activities. They do not expect to reach definitive, one-time conclusions, but rather to engage in a continuous process, making incremental advances, raising new hypotheses, gradually adding to the sum of knowledge about a particular issue. They expect that even empirical methodologies will change and improve over time, requiring new inquiries into old subjects as part of ongoing debates.[11] Thus, empirical legal scholars must be able switch analytical methods: they must teach their students to think like lawyers, but in scholarship must function as empiricists. For some decades, such mode switching was discouraged by hiring and tenure processes within the American legal academy.

In the latter part of the twentieth century, new theoretical schools such as critical legal studies, critical race theory, and feminist legal theory blossomed. As legal scholarship increasingly removed itself from legal practice, many American law professors came to see their role as philosopher-scholars, rather than pragmatic teachers of useful doctrines and practical arts. Practice skills were left to nontenured clinicians. Doctorates in nonlegal fields became valuable commodities in the difficult search for law school teaching positions. Peer pressures guided young scholars away from doctrinal or empirical work, likely to be damned as "merely descriptive," toward abstract theoretical scholarship. Given the bias in the academy, doctrinal or empirical work did not have "sex appeal" to the students who run the law reviews and journals that are the primary publication outlets for law professors. To engage in such scholarship was to relegate one's work to specialty journals or risk going unpublished altogether, thereby imperiling one's chances for tenure.

The academic concentration on theory insured that young lawyers were released to the world with few practice skills, rather as if medical students were approved for practice without any clinical experience in advising patients or treating viral infections. In copyright, as in other fields, the bias against descriptive work ensured that little scholarship, particularly by junior faculty, was devoted to detailed, factual studies of copyright systems. Interestingly, a parallel trend emerged in macroeconomics. Economists abandoned empirical work in favor of theoretical studies that reused the same existing data sets from the same few, wealthy countries.[12] Thus, while it would seem that law and economics scholars, in particular, should have been interested in quantifying the economic impacts of copyright law, little empirical work was done in that area.

Beginning in the 1990s, the focus of American law professors on abstract theory, to the exclusion of study of the actual effects of legal doctrine in practice,

---

[11] *See,* Robert M. Lawless, Jennifer K. Robbennolt, and Thomas S. Ulen, Empirical Methods in Law 10–17 (2010).

[12] Catherine Rampell, *They Did Their Homework (800 Years of It),* N.Y. Times, July 2, 2010, at BU1.

drew criticism from those engaged in the real world of legal practice.[13] Since the beginning of the new millennium, the disinclination to empirical and doctrinal work has reversed in the legal and economics academies and in copyright scholarship specifically. The empirical legal studies movement has begun to apply empirical methodologies to study of the legal system. An influential study of American legal education has called for better integration of cognitive, practical, and social-ethical training of lawyers.[14] Historical, empirical studies of economic boom and bust cycles are back in vogue.[15] Law professors and economists are taking a greater interest in empirical exploration of copyright industries and the impact of copyright law on culture as well as markets. The studies have taken several different forms: studies of particular "hot-button" issues; economic studies of the impact of copyright on creative production; broader studies not only exploring correlations between copyright law and creativity, but also looking for correlations between other factors and creative production, and studies of the historical development of copyright industries.

Recent Studies

The explosive impact of computer technologies and the Internet on the copyright ecosystem has increasingly engendered empirical studies in particularly controversial areas such as the effect of peer-to-peer file sharing on the recording industry. Oberholzer-Gee and Strumpf initially concluded that file sharing had little impact on CD sales, while Leibowitz came to the opposite conclusion.[16] Oberholzer-Gee and Strumpf subsequently reviewed varying methodologies as well as other studies and concluded that file sharing was responsible for, at most, 20% of the decline in CD sales.[17] That conclusion roughly matched the findings

---

13 *See, e.g.*, Harry T. Edwards, *The Growing Disjunction between Legal Education and the Legal Profession*, 91 MICH. L. REV. 34 (1992).

14 WILLIAM M. SULLIVAN, ANNE COLBY, JUDITH WELCH WAGNER, LLOYD BOND, AND LEE S. SHULMAN, EDUCATING LAWYERS: PREPARATION FOR THE PROFESSION OF LAW 191–202 (2007).

15 *See* Rampell, *supra* note 12.

16 *Compare* Stan J. Liebowitz, *Pitfalls in Measuring the Impact of File-Sharing on the Sound Recording Market*, 51 CESIFO ECON. STUD. 439 (2005), *available at* http://www.utdallas.edu/~liebowit/intprop/pitfalls.pdf (finding that file sharing adversely impacts sales), *with* Felix Oberholzer-Gee and Koleman Strumpf, *The Effect of File Sharing on Record Sales:An Empirical Analysis* (2004), http://www.unc.edu/~cigar/papers/FileSharing_March2004.pdf (finding no statistical correlation between file sharing and slumps in music sales).

17 Felix Oberholzer-Gee and Koleman Strumpf, *File-Sharing and Copyright* 1 (2010), http://musicbusinessresearch.files.wordpress.com/2010/06/paper-felix-oberholzer-gee.pdf.

of a separate study conducted in the United Kingdom in 2007.[18] The revised study also explored the impact of file sharing on musicians, citing data showing that record sales have relatively little impact on musical creativity.[19]

Additional limited studies focus on very short time frames and subject matters. For example, studies have examined the impact of pro-copyright legislative and judicial changes on market valuation of copyright firms from 1985–1998,[20] the impact of those changes on copyright applications in the same period,[21] and the impact of extension of copyright duration on movie production from 1991–2002.[22] While these studies are fairly limited in scope, broader studies of the impacts of copyright protections have also reassessed the utilitarian justification for copyright, with varying results.

By 2003, when Landes and Posner incorporated their work on the economics of copyright into the book *The Economic Structure of Intellectual Property Law*, they added analysis of a limited set of economic data regarding the impact of five changes in copyright law on the number of new works produced as gauged by increases or declines in copyright registrations.[23] Their limited data showed no statistically significant relationship between extensions in copyright's duration and the number of new works produced, though they continued to argue, pursuing the standard linear logic of copyright's past, that increased protection should produce more new works.[24] A more recent and comprehensive study challenges the connection between expanded copyright protections and increased production of works.

Raymond Shih Ray Ku, a law professor, collaborated with statisticians Jiayang Sun and Yiying Fan on a study analyzing how population, the economy, legislative and judicial changes in copyright law, and technology influenced new

---

18 Andrew Orlowski, *Apple, Tesco "Most to Blame" for Music Biz Crisis*, The Register (Oct. 19, 2007, 10:49 GMT), http://www.theregister.co.uk/2007/10/19/vrs_value_gap_report/.

19 Oberholzer-Gee and Strumpf, *supra* note 17, at 22–4.

20 *See* Matthew J. Baker and Brendan M. Cunningham, *Court Decisions and Equity Markets: Estimating the Value of Copyright Protection,* 49 J.L. & Econ. 567 (2006).

21 Matthew J. Baker and Brendan M. Cunningham, *Law and Innovation in Copyright Industries*, 6(1) Rev. Econ. Res. on Copyright Issues 61–82 (2009), *available at* http://ssrn.com/abstract=1436160.

22 Ivan P.L. Png and Qiu-Hong Wang, *Copyright Duration and the Supply of Creative Work* 1 (Sept. 2006), http:// papers.ssrn.com/sol3/papers.cfm?abstract_id=932161.

23 *See* William M. Landes and Richard A. Posner, The Economic Structure of Intellectual Property Law 234–49 (2003).

24 *Id.*, at 247.

copyright registrations from 1870 to 2006. Analyzing this larger set of factors, they tested the hypothesis that any change in copyright law would change the number of works produced and the related hypotheses that increasing copyright protection increases the number of works produced while decreasing copyright protection reduces the number of works produced. Their conclusion: the data did not support the argument that increased copyright protection produced an increase in the number of copyrighted works produced. Rather, the long-term growth in the number of copyrighted works correlated to increased population, and sharp changes in the number of registrations correlated primarily to procedural changes in registration requirements.[25] To the extent that a correlation did exist between changes in copyright law and registrations, the data indicated that limitations on copyright protection, not expansions, were more likely to increase registrations of copyrighted works. Oberholzer-Gee and Strumpf note a similar phenomenon globally—the looser the copyright regime, the higher copyright production. Despite file sharing and other forms of piracy, production of copyrighted works has continued to increase in recent years.[26]

Scholars have also produced historical studies that evaluate the linkage between legal protection and copyright industry development. Studies of historical data on classical music production in the eighteenth century seem to indicate that the creation of copyright to protect such music had little impact on actual production.[27] Economists Michele Boldrin and David K. Levine compiled historical data about various copyright industries to demonstrate that many such industries developed without the benefit of copyright protection or, indeed, in defiance of it. The software, movie, and recording industries, for example, were born and prospered largely without copyright protection, which was nonetheless conferred on them after they gained significant economic and political strength.[28] Such findings suggest that copyright law often reacts to the development of markets in expressive works rather than stimulating the production of such works.

Boldrin and Levine also compiled developmental data that cast general doubt on the efficacy of intellectual monopoly laws like copyright to incentivize creation and, in fact, suggest that such laws may repress rather than encourage

---

25 Raymond Shih Ray Ku, Jiayang Sun, and Yiying Fan, *Does Copyright Law Promote Creativity? An Empirical Analysis of Copyright's Bounty*, 62 Vand. L. Rev. 1669, 1671–72 (2009).

26 Oberholzer-Gee and Strumpf, *supra* note 17, at 24.

27 Michele Boldrin and David K. Levine, Against Intellectual Monopoly 187–9 (2008).

28 *Id.*, at 15–39.

innovation.[29] For example, in the United States, now the most vocal proponent of strong copyright, much of the current copyright infrastructure was built by virtue of flagrant piracy when the U.S was a net importer of cultural artifacts rather than an exporter of them.[30] China and other developing countries seem to be following a similar pattern. More extensive studies might indicate that developing countries naturally follow a cycle in which "piracy" contributes to development up to some definable point at which the government begins to impose and enforce stronger copyright laws in order to protect newly established industries. Alternatively, the move to strong copyrights may reflect no more than the increased political influence of copyright industries who are certainly not averse to gaining monopoly power even where such power may not be essential to their survival.

In a recent book comparing industrialization in England and Germany, economic historian Eckhard Hoffner makes an even bolder assertion: that Germany's rapid industrial expansion in the 1800s was actually attributable to its *lack* of copyright law, which permitted widespread, inexpensive circulation of the latest works of scientific information. Relying on empirical data showing the number of publications in Germany and Britain, he suggests that strong copyright monopolies in Britain substantially slowed the dissemination of such information, and cost Britain its initial advantage in industrialization.[31] Historical studies have also disproved claims that new technologies necessarily have adverse impacts on preexisting copyright industries. True, some copyright-related industries have failed to adapt to changing technologies. Congress is no longer concerned about a monopoly in production of player piano rolls, for example. History shows, however, that established industries often co-opted and benefited from new technologies, finding new revenue streams in new media.[32] Each of the studies just described is valuable within its own self-defined sphere, yet much more could be done to enhance our understanding of the copyright ecosystem and copyright law's contribution to its sustainability. The need for such analysis becomes more pressing as copyright law in the digital environment has increasingly direct impacts on individual consumers.

---

29 *Id.*, at 208.

30 *Id.*, at 23.

31 Frank Thadeusz, *No Copyright Law: the Real Reason for Germany's Industrial Expansion*?, Spiegel online (Aug. 18, 2010, 4:52 PM), http://www.spiegel.de/international/zeitgeist/0,1518,druck-710976,00.html.

32 *Network Effects: How a New Communications Technology Disrupted America's newspaper industry—in 1845,* The Economist, Dec. 19, 2009, at 142–4.

The Users' Dilemma

The arcane body of copyright law developed primarily in the context of disputes between commercial enterprises. Those businesses were represented by specialized attorneys familiar with the workings of the industries and the Byzantine convolutions of laws partially drafted by those industries. In the analog world, ordinary users of copyrighted works lived their lives at a happy remove from such legal complications, rarely coming into direct contact with copyright law. Certainly, they were involved in activities that copyright owners considered to be infringement, such as creating mix tapes, recording television shows off the air, photocopying and distribution of favorite comics or poems or articles, or the unauthorized performance of copyrighted songs at birthday parties or around the campfire.

However, the copies were imperfect and had little impact on copyright holders' markets, and users' activities were difficult to detect. While overzealous copyright owners might occasionally threaten Girl Scout camps over campfire tunes, or day care centers over cartoon murals,[33] pursuit of individual users was hardly worth the cost, or the adverse public relations consequences. In the digital world, that economic calculus changed dramatically as the same technological changes that made vast quantities of information readily available and empowered users to manipulate them also brought into the spotlight user sharing activities that might constitute infringement.

The combination of affordable home computers with broadband Internet connections worked a sea change in the ways that users interacted with copyrighted material. Personal computers gave users the capability to make not just copies, but perfect, easily transmissible copies, of most kinds of copyrighted content. The Internet and the World Wide Web provided users with a comprehensive, easy to use system for both acquiring and further distributing copyrighted works. As file compression and file sharing technologies rapidly improved, user's capabilities came to pose a significant threat to copyright owners' markets. Their activities also became more readily detectable by copyright owners, who can now trace potentially infringing activities at least as far as a computer Internet Protocol (IP) address and sometimes as far as the actual identity of the person sitting in front of

[33] No kidding. *See* "*Cartoon Figures Run Afoul of Law*," Chi. Trib., 27 Apr. 1989, at 26 (Disney demanded that the day care centers paint over the murals); Elizabeth Bumiller, *Battle Hymns around Campfires; ASCAP Asks Royalties from Girl Scouts, and Regrets it*, N.Y. Times, Dec. 17, 1996, at 1 (ASCAP ultimately backed off its claim to royalties). Both enforcement attempts were public relations disasters for the copyright owners.

the computer screen. More importantly, owners now have significant incentive to track individual infringers because user sharing activities have direct, potentially disastrous impact on the industries' bottom lines.

The sound recording industry felt the earliest impacts. Despite their desperate, and sometimes misguided, efforts to quell user infringements, it has become increasingly clear that the industry, in its existing form, is seriously threatened by user activities. Other content industries now face similar problems. Suits against individual file sharers, recently abandoned, represented an entirely new front in the war against infringement—one that put individual users in the line of fire for the first time. Three strikes laws depriving alleged infringers of Internet access, proposals for laptop searches at borders, and the like, directly impact ordinary users. Increasingly strong enforcement may also adversely impact future creators. Copyright now collides with our common culture. We must know more about how the industries, social networks, electronic technologies, and copyright law interact in the real world if we are to calibrate laws for this new electronic environment.

Uses for Empirical Research

Obviously, any empirical approach, even those not based in complexity theory, permits testing of the assumed linkages between copyright incentives, creativity, and public access embodied in the utilitarian framework for copyright. Researchers can investigate the changes in surrounding environments that have triggered legislative and judicial changes in copyright law over time. They can ask how the law responded to those changes and look for causal relationships between legal responses and the production of works. They can question whether copyright law achieves its utilitarian goals of encouraging creativity and promoting "the Progress of Science and useful Arts." Researchers might survey creators to inquire whether they are, in fact, motivated in whole or in part by the legal protections conferred on them by copyright. Utilitarian theory, tied as it is to economic incentives, invites such inquiries. Personhood and labor theory, based on moral assumptions, nonetheless admit of some empirical testing. Researchers testing labor theory might examine, for example, whether the reward conferred by copyright law is actually commensurate to the labor invested.

In addition to testing the existing theoretical justifications for copyright protection, any empirical approach permits evaluation of particular arguments often employed in support of the efforts to expand or curtail copyright and related laws. For example, the copyright industries have long argued that the success of mass-market works, like blockbuster movies, novels, or Top 40 pop hits, subsidizes their production and distribution of less popular, but culturally valuable works. A Stephen King novel, the argument suggests, gives its publisher the wherewithal to put out collected essays or poetry or short stories by less popular authors. A best selling album by Madonna subsidizes jazz or classical recordings. Copyright industries also argue that the massive profits from the blockbusters cover the losses for works that simply fail to find an audience at all, such as the box office flop that costs millions to make but never turns a profit. On the other side of the debate, low protectionists assert that the expansion of copyright constricts the public domain, and thereby limits the production of new works by preventing access to essential cultural building blocks. Such assertions can, and should, be tested.

Many of the studies done thus far focus on the market aspects of copyright, counting dollars or widgets produced, in the form of registered works, as proxies for creative production. More work is needed, exploring other variables that may affect creativity and firmly placing copyright systems in the larger context of their social, as well as economic, environments. Complexity theory and a systems approach offer a framework and methodology for investigation that, unlike traditional economic analyses, takes into account the many interactions among the economic, social, political, and technology systems that produce our present copyright environment. The remainder of the chapter sketches out possible complexity-based approaches to empirical studies of copyright. Much of it is highly speculative—a first attempt to think through applications for complexity theory in a context where little such work has previously been done.

Outlining a Systems Approach to Copyright

In general terms, a systems approach to any subject of study must be holistic, rather than reductive. In complex adaptive systems, long-term patterns of behavior emerge from a comprehensive web of interconnections and interactions. Any student of such systems must not merely gain an understanding of their constituent parts but must also understand the full panoply of emergent patterns, relationships, and adaptive behaviors inherently generated by the interactions among those parts and among different systems. Thus, analysis of individual components of complex adaptive systems is necessary, but not sufficient to provide a complete understanding of the systems. Studies of individual bees will not capture the swarm logic of the hive. Studies of the biology of grasses may not capture the importance of fire to the prairie ecosystem. Rather, a researcher must study the system at "landscape scale" in order to capture its emergent and coevolutionary properties.[34] Because many complex adaptive systems nest within and interact with each other, careful definition of the system to be studied can be both critical and difficult. System definition may vary dependent on the purpose of the research. Researchers must also be careful not to manipulate the definition in ways that could skew the results.

Defining and Mapping the Systems

When analyzing human-created systems like copyright systems, one might start by identifying the broad goals of a particular system. What was it made to do? The goals of copyright law, as stated in the Constitution and statutes, are to encourage the creation of new works by rewarding authors and publishers and to enrich and disseminate the common culture. Goals of particular players in the copyright ecosystem may be somewhat harder to pin down, though the general aims of such players may be self-evident. Some of the goals of the sound recording industry, for example, might be stated as: discovery of talented songwriters and performers, creation of sound recordings, promotion through advertising of both performers and recordings, and the making of a reasonable profit on those activities in order to continue to perform them. Qualitative surveys of industry professionals might help to refine the statement of system goals for particular systems. The goals of the system offer a starting point for charting its boundaries.

Once the goals are defined, the researcher can begin the process of describing and mapping the components and processes that contribute to, or possibly detract from, the achievement of the system's goals. Researchers should chart and, where possible, quantify the inputs and outputs of the system, the flows, linkages, and feedback loops in the system's processes. They should identify the rules of interaction that govern those processes. In other words, the researcher should produce a map of the system—essentially a system flow chart—much as a programmer charts the process flows of a software program. Any such descriptive map must also take into account influences exerted by other systems with which the target system interacts: inputs may depend on outside sources; outputs often flow outside the system; rules may be imposed both within and from without, and the system will coevolve with other significant systems in its environment.

In other words, the researcher must map out not only the internal workings of the system, but its interactions with other systems, in order to achieve a landscape-

34 J.B. Ruhl, *Law's Complexity: A Primer*, 24 GA. ST. U. L. REV. 885, 894 (2008).

scale view of the system. Circumscribing the boundaries of the target system may be relatively easy in some cases, but may require difficult choices in others. Where, for example, does the recording industry stop and the music distribution system begin? Descriptive work of this nature, far from being without value, sets the stage for more in-depth inquiry.

Obviously, this sort of mapping process makes the most sense with respect to physical copyright systems like the industries that produce or disseminate copyrighted works. Those systems may more readily be defined and described than the conceptual aspects of copyright law itself. They contain the kinds of components, processes, and flows that lend themselves to mapping. Researchers can map industry inputs, such as money, information, labor, and materials, whether those inputs are monetized or nonmonetized. They can chart the process flows within each industry and the outputs that result in the form of copyrightable works or other products. Internal maps will differ for different kinds of works within those industries; for example, the processes that produce mass-market novels may vary from those that produce academic works or poetry. Mapping cannot, however, be limited to internal processes within the target system but must also reflect interactions with other systems.

A systems approach to copyright requires that an investigator consider not only the economic factors typically considered in empirical work, but also the social networks and technological systems that impact the system. For example, blockbuster phenomena, like the Potter series or the *Lord of the Rings* trilogy, straddle mutually interacting industries and depend not only on the industries that produce them but also on the emergence of fan networks that boost them by the electronic equivalent of "word of mouth" and the analog and digital technologies that make them available to their fan base. Assessment of the impact of music file sharing on sound recording production requires not only analysis of recording industry receipts but also attention to the emergence of social sharing norms and the technologies that both facilitate such sharing and offer alternative channels of distribution to artists. Such interactions must be as thoroughly considered as the economic factors.

Frameworks, Models, and Data

Once the target system is defined and mapped, the researcher can begin to generate and test hypotheses about the system, determine which factors are most critical to its functions, and assess the impacts of alterations in its rules or its environment. In order to do so, the researcher must essentially put the static system map into motion over time since evolution and emergence are the essence of complex adaptive systems. Researchers in other fields, operating within the general framework of complexity theory, typically create models of the interactions among system agents to simplify this analysis. In an article regarding complexity modeling of legal systems, J.B. Ruhl suggests that, unlike typical social science models which focus on either very few agents (often two) or very many agents whose actions can be averaged, complexity models should reflect the moderate-number contexts in which most economic, legal, social, and political interactions occur.[35] Complexity models are also probabilistic and more likely to reveal power law distributions than linear, proportional relationships between causes and effects. Thus, such models should have some predictive value, though their predictions would likely be within a range of possibilities—more like a weather forecast than a revenue forecast.

Elinor Ostrom and Charlotte Hess have proposed the use of a general framework that might facilitate the creation of specific models for particular copyright systems. They suggest that information should be treated as a shared knowledge commons, a complex information ecosystem that presents certain social dilemmas.[36] They recommend adoption of the Institutional Analysis and Development (IAD) framework to investigate any subject matter where humans repeatedly interact within rules and norms that guide their choices of behavior.[37] Ostrom and Hess argue that the framework is well adapted to analysis of various types of commons or common-pool resources like information, particularly where new technologies are rapidly developing and institutional change is occurring.[38] Using this framework, which focuses on institutions, Ostrom has produced empirical studies of management of common-pool resources, such as fisheries, forests, water resources, and grazing lands.[39]

The Ostrom-Hess elaboration of the IAD framework for the knowledge commons is clearly influenced by, and incorporates many salient aspects of, complexity theory. It recognizes that institutions comprise both formal and

---

35 *Id.*, at 889–90.

36 Charlotte Hess and Elinor Ostrom, *Introduction: an Overview of the Knowledge Commons*, in CHARLOTTE HESS AND ELINOR OSTROM, UNDERSTANDING KNOWLEDGE AS A COMMONS: FROM THEORY TO PRACTICE 3–14 (2007).

37 Charlotte Hess Elinor Ostrom, *A Framework for Analyzing the Knowledge Commons*, in CHARLOTTE HESS AND ELINOR OSTROM, UNDERSTANDING KNOWLEDGE AS A COMMONS: FROM THEORY TO PRACTICE 41 (2007).

38 *Id.*, at 43.

39 ELINOR OSTROM, GOVERNING THE COMMONS; THE EVOLUTION OF INSTITUTIONS FOR COLLECTIVE ACTION 29–38 (1990).

informal rules and focuses on how humans create organizations and make rules and decisions in order to sustain a resource or achieve an outcome. It recognizes that such arrangements will be dynamic and, accordingly, the methodology must also be fluid. The framework recognizes institutional "nestedness" and requires attention to the physical characteristics of the resource, definition of community attributes, studies of formal and normative rules in use at different levels of rulemaking, observation of patterns of interaction, and requirements for adaptive governance in a complex system.[40]

The framework remains couched in the language of commons philosophy and specifically focuses on institutional design. It is not meant to provide actual models of specific copyright systems. Ostrom and Hess apply the IAD framework to the creation of university digital repositories for scholarship as an example of how the framework might operate to produce a model of a specific commons project. Such a framework may provide a starting point for comprehensive empirical studies of the kind recommended herein, though it seems unlikely to serve as an analytical tool for all copyright systems and situations. Some tweaking may be required for some situations; other complexity-based frameworks may prove more viable for some studies. Indeed, several legal scholars have already proposed adaptations to the Ostrom–Hess model.[41] Moreover, at some point, any theoretical framework must be tethered to the reality of copyright systems operating in the current digital environment.

Complexity models created for copyright systems are likely to be specific and differentiated, not reflections of the simple binary "private property versus commons" philosophical framework currently dominant in copyright analysis. One single model is no more likely to apply to the panoply of copyright systems than the same complexity model would be to apply to a prairie and an old-growth forest. The movie industry employs different means of production and distribution than does the recording industry, though it faces similar challenges from digital media. Broadcast television differs from broadcast radio; the needs of developers of business software may differ significantly from those of video game makers. Similarly, copyright doctrines vary from context to context. The common law countries often take a different approach to copyright issues such as corporate ownership, moral rights, or the originality standard than do countries following a civil law tradition. Their respective approaches result from different paths taken

---

40 Hess and Ostrom, *supra* note 37, at 41–68.

41 *See* Michael J. Madison, Brett M. Frischmann, and Katherine J. Strandburg, *Constructing Commons in the Cultural Environment,* 95 CORNELL L. REV. 657 (2010) (proposing a variation on the framework, at a fairly high level of abstraction).

during the historical development of copyright law in their different legal cultures. Once a researcher settles on a model for chosen system, he must test it against proven realities. Building from empirical data up, rather than from commons theory down, may be the most effective approach in the long run.

Complexity scholars test their models by examining the actual behavior of the complex adaptive system being studied, whether the system is a stock market or an ecosystem. They continuously revise their models based on empirical data compiled over time to either support or invalidate particular hypotheses, in a process that is iterative and cumulative. Their research purposes may be to accurately describe a system, or to identify certain causal relationships between phenomena, or to trace evolutionary changes occurring over time. Similarly, copyright researchers employing a complexity framework should compile the data necessary to assess how, and whether, targeted copyright systems achieve their stated goals and the probable impact on them of changes in their environments, most recently the migration from analog to digital media. Researchers could examine associations between technological change and the industries and the copyright laws governing them. They might trace the evolution of a particular industry, of the copyright regime as a whole, or of particular copyright doctrines over time. Certainly, they should explore the impact of changes in copyright law on specific industries or on creative production in general, as the Ku-Sun-Fan study does.

Research Targets and Approaches

The copyright ecosystem contains a variety of subsystems that might, once properly defined, be targeted for study using a complexity framework. The copyright industries are certainly obvious targets. Studies that comprehensively map the workings of such industries, situate them in the broader context of their social, political, or economic environments, and quantify the actual impacts of copyright law on them have been rare in the legal literature. Scholars could, for example, update Breyer's study of book publishing, including new formats like the e-book, and examining the impact of changes in copyright law on the industry. They might investigate less well-known specialty industries like those that produce textbooks, academic scholarship, or legal materials. Scholars might compare alternative distributional networks such as bricks-and-mortar stores, online sellers like iTunes, or peer-to-peer file sharing. In doing so, they could test one of the longstanding justifications for copyright: that even if it is not necessary to induce creation, it is certainly necessary to support dissemination of works to the public. Do the data support this seemingly logical connection between copyright and dissemination?

And, if so, should copyright protection change if new electronic technologies permit direct, widespread distribution by the performer to her consumers?

The legal regime should face the same comprehensive scrutiny as the industries. New copyright doctrines do not appear out of thin air but are generated by changes in the economic, social, technological, and political environments. These interactions can be captured. The emergence of particular doctrines, the contexts in which they emerge, the inputs into the legislative and judicial processes that produce them, and their impacts, or lack thereof, on the production of copyrighted works can all be scrutinized and, insofar as possible, mapped out. Scholars might, for example, analyze the development and impact of doctrines relating to corporate ownership of creative works, their connection to the rise of corporations, and differing legal treatments in common law and civil law countries. They might compare the effectiveness of the different approaches based on their measurable impact on production of copyrighted works. Scholars might compare and contrast differing doctrinal treatments of particular copyright subject matter such as sound recordings or fashion in common and civil law countries. One might more generally expect to capture the influence of the copyright industries on legislators and courts, the role of precedent, the effect of the differing philosophical approaches of the common law and civil law traditions. The systems approach offers the opportunity for more comprehensive models of the empirical reality within which copyright decisions are made.

Significant legal copyright scholarship already exists that traces the history of copyright law,[42] often with reference to the social or political contexts in which the law evolved. Comparative legal scholarship contrasts copyright developments in different countries or regions such as the divergence between common law and civil law countries with regard to the moral rights of authors. A systems approach could certainly encompass these basic empirical methodologies and make use of the data points they reveal. Researchers would compile and analyze historical and comparative data about target systems and would certainly collect data on industry costs, revenues, and profits. Where industries obtain new copyright protections, such data would provide a base to which later researchers might refer to determine the impact of particular copyright legislation. However, the complexity researcher must go beyond economic analysis of costs, returns, and profits. Many essential elements of copyright systems come without a price tag attached. The mapping and data collection processes should also, for example, capture inputs like public

---

[42] *See, e.g.*, L. Ray Patterson and Stanley W. Lindberg, The Nature of Copyright: A Law of Users' Rights (1991).

domain information that are basically free to the industry but important to its survival. By mapping out flows of information, systems analysis may also capture nonmonetizable factors such as public access to information that traditional economic analyses fail to take into account.

Copyright scholars have long recognized that the public domain provides essential materials for the creation of new copyrightable works. Doctrines preventing copyright in ideas or facts and allowing fair use (or fair dealing) specifically protect the public domain, as durational limits once did, in order to ensure the availability of those inputs to future authors. Some industries profit directly by organizing publicly available information. Publishers of legal information, for example, have built thriving empires by consolidating, improving, and packaging information that is largely in the public domain. Newspapers package and disseminate facts. *All* copyrighted works build on elements from the public domain to some extent, whether that information takes the form of shared culture or of preexisting works incorporating that culture.

Consider, for example, how many elements of Rowling's Harry Potter books depend on common cultural understandings accumulated over centuries: witches and wizards, wands and spells, flying broomsticks, trolls, giants, centaurs, the English boarding school environment. Like most authors, Rowling draws on shared mythologies and inventively repurposes them to create new works. J.R.R. Tolkien used many similar cultural elements, to very different effect, in *The Hobbit* and *The Lord of the Rings*, and it seems likely that Rowling's later works are influenced by the works of Tolkien as well as those of other writers. Shakespeare wrote plays relying on others' works of history, as well as on tales of woodland sprites and ghosts, transforming them into one of the greatest bodies of literary work ever produced. Keats was inspired by the design of ancient Greek urns and the myth of the lamia. The public domain is an essential input for all copyright systems.

Equally, the outputs of copyright industries often feed into the culture both before and after the copyright expires. Every creator draws from the cultural pool and then contributes back into it—to each according to his need, from each according to her talent. Themes, tropes, memes, mythologies are created, disseminated, modified, renewed, and recycled in continuous feedback loops that, over time, build our culture. The audience, as well as the author, contributes to the process. A holistic approach to the study of copyright requires recognition of these cycles. Copyright systems involve interdependent, dynamic processes, not merely discrete sets of products. With new techniques of statistical analysis, researchers might even be able to produce quantifications of the extent to which new, copyrighted works depend on and incorporate public domain information and common cultural knowledge.

Researchers now use large-scale quantitative analysis in fields formerly immune to statistical inquiry. Historians of science count the incidence of certain key words in Victorian book titles as a means to challenge or verify claims about Victorian beliefs.[43] Scientists are devising tests to quantify what makes music expressive.[44] Ecologists have recently created a system for measuring the nonmonetizable contributions that rainforests make to carbon sequestration, prevention of natural hazards like landslides, eco-tourism and the like.[45] Perhaps similar queries, enabled by modern computing power, could track and quantify the appearance of public domain information in copyrighted works or trace the development of memes in our common culture. The public domain is our cultural rainforest. Measuring only the commercial value of works is like counting only the value of the lumber in the rainforest without counting its contribution to the global atmosphere. Moreover, digital statistics can now be transformed into visual maps and graphs. In the digital humanities, researchers map the travels of Thomas Jefferson, or the influence of collaborations on jazz, or the flow of ideas during the Enlightenment as represented in the letters of Locke, Newton, and Voltaire.[46] Scientists map traffic patterns on the Internet.[47] As researchers accumulate empirical data on all kinds of copyright systems, we can map those systems in ways never previously possible. Perhaps we can even look forward to bubble graph animations, based on statistical models, which trace the rise and fall of creative production as statistician Hans Rosling now uses bubble graph software to visually demonstrate the developmental progress of nations.[48]

There will always remain some elements of creative expression that are simply not amenable to quantitative analysis. Some values cannot be measured precisely because they involve moral judgments about, for example, the ethics

---

43 Patricia Cohen, *Analyzing Literature by Words, but also by the Numbers*, N.Y.Times, Dec. 4, 2010, at C1.

44 Pam Belluck, *To Tug at the Heart, Music First Must Tickle the Neurons*, N.Y. Times, Apr. 18, 2011, at D1.

45 *Money can Grow on Trees: Forests are Disappearing Because They are Undervalued*, The Economist, Sept. 25, 2010, at 6, 7, *available at* http://www.economist.com/node/17062651.

46 Patricia Cohen, *Humanities 2.0: A New Enlightenment: Digital Keys to the Humanities' Riches*, N.Y. Times, Nov. 17, 2010, at C1.

47 John Markoff, *Striving to Map the Shape-Shifting Net*, N.Y. Times, Mar. 1, 2010, at D1.

48 *Making Data Dance*, The Economist Tech. Q., Dec. 11, 2010, at 25, 26.

of plagiarizing others' work. Here qualitative research into the behavior of system actors might prove invaluable in establishing the motivations of creators and industry professionals or the attitudes of users toward copying the work of others or towards copyright law itself. One researcher has already embarked on such a study, interviewing creators and innovators in many fields, their business managers, IP lawyers, and other industry professionals in an attempt to describe creative processes and the motivations for them. She intends to apply qualitative textual analysis to the transcripts of the interviews in order to derive a systematic understanding of the popular legal consciousness regarding IP.[49] Similar work should provide useful data, while recognizing that not all values can be reduced to dollars and cents.

Economic analyses will, of course, remain important to any understanding of copyright law, which has avowedly economic underpinnings particularly in the common law tradition. Economic analysis is necessary because it explains a significant set of components and processes involved in such systems, but it is not sufficient to capture the full complexity of the copyright universe. The "dismal science" reduces much of human endeavor to a matter of dollars and cents, gain and loss, stripping it of less readily quantifiable human qualities like altruism, sharing, concerns with justice, satisfactions derived from noneconomic activities. Similarly, studies focused only on the economics of copyright miss critical elements important to copyright, creativity, and culture. The utilitarian focus on economic incentives has obscured other values inherent in copyright, such as the importance of artistic diversity and semiotic democracy. An effective copyright analyst must observe not just particular markets, but the social and political networks and the technological systems that surround them, in order to produce coherent models of the operation of various copyright systems and the impact on them of copyright law.

Advantages over Standard Economic Analysis

The systems approach has several advantages as compared to standard law and economics analysis. It encompasses factors, such as unpaid information creation and dissemination, social norms, and technological change, often missed in standard cost–benefit analyses that focus exclusively on markets. A systems approach recognizes that copyright systems are interdependent and dynamic, adapting to changing environments over time in behavioral patterns that are

[49] Jessica Silbey, *Harvesting Intellectual Property, Abstract*, http://ssrn.com/abstract=1599747.

likely to be nonlinear and unpredictable. Cost–benefit analysis, like the utilitarian assumption that copyright protection assures production, assumes linear cause–effect relationships that may pertain in the short term, but will not obtain in the long term in complex adaptive systems. Indeed, the Ku-Sun-Fan study found no statistically significant directional relationship between expansions of copyright protection and registration of new copyrights, concluding that the probable response to legal changes was hard to predict—as one would expect in any complex adaptive system.[50]

Complexity researchers must challenge the assumptions of traditional economics when those assumptions are unsupported by data. Some of the foundational precepts of traditional equilibrium economics are manifestly at odds with reality. Traditional economics assumes, for example, that economic actors always act rationally to maximize their wealth. The history of boom-and-bust cycles in markets has shown, however, that economic actors behave far from rationally as emergent aggregate patterns of behavior first inflate investments in rare tulip bulbs or McMansions, then rapidly deflate their value when the bubble is finally pricked. The Ku-Sun-Fan study points out that, given the known costs of producing copyrighted works and the uncertainty that a work from a new author will find a market that returns a profit, no rational wealth maximizer would ever engage in what is, in effect, a lottery.[51] Such phenomena illustrate complexity at work, and emerging economic disciplines have begun to challenge the traditional economic paradigm.

Behavioral economics and game theory challenge the traditional view of strategic economic behavior.[52] Complexity economists[53] and ecological economists[54] have formulated evolutionary approaches that recognize inherent resource limitations in economic systems. With the recent implosion of the financial system, critics have

---

[50] Ku et al., *supra* note 25, at 1694, 1712.

[51] Ku et al., *supra* note 25, at 1713–19. The authors elaborate on several other omissions in the traditional economic model of copyright.

[52] *See, e.g.*, Craig Lambert, *The Marketplace of Perceptions: Behavioral Economics Explains Why We Procrastinate, Buy, and Grab Chocolate on the Spur of the Moment*, Harvard Magazine, Mar.–Apr. 2006, at 50–57.

[53] *See, e.g.*, Eric. D. Beinhocker, The Origin of Wealth: Evolution, Complexity, and the Radical Remaking of Economics (2006) (describing economies as adaptive systems that evolve in response to technological innovation, social development and business practices).

[54] *See, e.g.*, Joshua Farley, Ecological Economics: Principles and Applications (2003) (describing an interdisciplinary framework for economics that recognizes linkages among economic growth, environmental degradation, and social inequity).

blasted the "dynamic stochastic general equilibrium model" used by the Federal Reserve and other central banks as well as the assumptions of efficient financial markets and rational behavior on which the models are predicated. Economists have begun to explore "agent-based modeling" using a bottom-up approach in which agents interact directly with each other, rather than responding merely to price. They make no assumption of market efficiency or movement toward equilibrium. These nonlinear models recognize the interactions between different economic sectors and generate model markets that look like weather systems, incorporating fluctuations and crashes, feedback mechanisms that amplify effects such as investor "herding" and panics, and network-based vulnerabilities created by complex derivatives.[55] The study of economics itself, then, is bending toward complexity theory in ways not yet fully absorbed by the law and economics school. The newly emerging economic disciplines can contribute important insights into the operations of copyright systems.

What Will We Find?

The end results of complexity studies are likely to be as differentiated and variable as the models employed. Empirical data may indicate that copyright incentives are necessary for some kinds of works, but not others, or that legal incentives are needed for dissemination, but not necessarily creation of some kinds of works. Changing technologies may eliminate the need for copyright incentives to some copyright actors. It has been suggested, for example, that the ease of distribution of sound recordings over the Internet eliminates the need for copyright incentives to studios, whose primary role has become the marketing of recordings rather than their actual production.[56] The Ku-Sun-Fan study paints a complex picture of the effect of changes in copyright law on copyright registrations, if not actual productivity. Their work indicates that the impact varies for different types of works, with some being more sensitive to legal change than others. Impact also depends on the type of legal change. Their data indicate that laws limiting or decreasing copyright are more likely to be associated with increases in registrations than laws expanding copyright protections.[57] Such variability with regard to the impact of legal incentives may require a more tailored approach to copyright law-making.

---

[55] *Economics focus: Agents of Change,* The Economist, July 24, 2010, at 76.

[56] *See* Raymond Shih Ray Ku, *The Creative Destruction Of Copyright: Napster And The New Economics Of Digital Technology,* 69 U. Chi. L. Rev. 263 (2002).

[57] Ku *et al.*, *supra* note 25, at 1708–12.

Different means of allocating rights in information may be shown to be more productive than the current division between private ownership and the public domain. The work of Ostrom and others on the impact of human interactions on the sustainability of ecosystems suggests that there are workable institutional alternatives to individual private ownership or entirely public ownership of resources. Villages in Switzerland and Japan have regulated communally owned lands successfully for centuries. Other communities around the world have successfully managed irrigation rights.[58] Studies of fishing rights have shown that fisheries may be sustainably managed by groups of people who hold long-term, fixed shares in the catch, giving them an incentive to protect and grow the resource.[59] Perhaps such communal ownership models could be adapted to the information ecosystem for purposes of establishing the parameters of ownership in communally produced information. Such a model might mitigate in favor of tribal rights in traditional knowledge and folklore, for example. It might prove useful with respect to the increasing number of digital works produced by loose collectives of creators in the form of wikis or blogs.

If empirical research establishes considerable variation among the response of different copyright systems to legal change, lawmakers may wish to consider more carefully their strategies for guiding copyright systems through the use of law. One size-fits-all copyright laws may not, in all cases, achieve the desired goals. Nonetheless, it seems likely that, as more studies are done and data accumulate at the landscape scale, emergent patterns that cut across copyright systems will also become evident. The data may reveal commonalities as well as differences among certain systems. Those commonalties may enable the use of generalized legal rules in some situations. Empirical work would provide a basis for a more nuanced approach toward devising a legal regime that will keep creative systems sustainable. Such a regime must be more flexible, and more attuned to realities on the ground, than the binary model.

Roadblocks

The systems approach to copyright faces a number of roadblocks. It will, for one thing, require interdisciplinary cooperation among collaborators in a variety of disciplines, which may include not only law and economics, but also statistics,

---

58 Ostrom, *supra* note 35, at 61–88.

59 Aaron E. Hirsh, *Guest Column: Fish Shares and Sharing Fish*, N.Y. Times, The Wild Side, Feb. 3, 2009 (10:00 PM); Bryan Walsh, *Sustainable Sushi*, TIME, Oct. 27, 2008, at 56.

cognitive sciences, business methods, and political science to name a few. Copyright law scholars are likely to require the support of statisticians, as, for example, in the Ku-Sun-Fan collaborative study. Modern copyright systems are global in scope, so collaboration may often be transnational as well as transdisciplinary. Such collaborations will inevitably face the logistical problems typically associated with the coordination of activities by multiple actors in a variety of locations over time.

The accumulation of comprehensive data, much less its analysis, will require rather substantial periods of time and must be viewed as an ongoing process. Good data may be easy to come by for some systems, but very difficult to acquire for others. Perfect information is unlikely to be available even where empirical work is feasible. Some industries may resist the release of data about their workings if they believe that the data would put them at a strategic disadvantage vis-à-vis their competitors or prevent them from acquiring legal protections that they desire. Given the complexity of the systems studied, the researchers will have to make some hard choices about the factors to be considered and methodologies to be used. Researchers will have to be knowledgeable about their subject in order simply to set up the parameters of their study. They must make judgments about which legal changes are significant enough to be included, whether to treat legislative changes differently than judicial changes, how to identify the significant technological changes. They must consider social factors like population growth, urbanization, and social networking. It may be difficult, or impossible, to develop models that can account for or measure all critical factors.

Using copyright registrations as a proxy for copyrighted works produced, for example, omits the undoubtedly large number of works that are created, but never registered. Under current law, those works are nonetheless copyrighted as soon as they are captured in a tangible medium of expression, so studies like the Landes-Posner and Ku-Sun-Fan studies will miss part of the picture by relying on registrations as a proxy for creation. Researchers will also have to sort out the many factors that may contribute to a certain result. For example, changes in the level of copyright registrations cannot be connected to temporally concurrent changes in technologies without accounting for other factors, such as procedural changes in registration policies or population growth, that also impact registrations.[60]

Even after data have been acquired and analyzed on particular issues, disputes will arise over methodologies, data reliability, and interpretation. The Landes-Posner and Ku-Sun-Fan studies reach different conclusions that may be explained

[60] Ku et al., *supra* note 25, at 1679–80.

by the different data sets and procedures they used. As noted above, early studies on the effect of file sharing on CD sales reached markedly different conclusions, which then, over time, started to converge more closely. Such disputes are to be expected as part of any empirical process. As methodologies improve and data accumulate, the weight of the findings will eventually resolve issues. As the case of the recording industry demonstrates, copyright systems will continue to evolve, in some cases quite rapidly, even as researchers study them. The description and analysis of those changes, in themselves, offer valuable information about the systems and their adaptability to social and technological change, creating an informational feedback loop.

Conclusion

Taken collectively, the systemic studies described above might finally allow us to evaluate copyright law as a conceptual system designed to guide the information ecosystem that sustains our cultures and a substantial chunk of the global economy. They would provide us with the data we need to determine whether copyright functions, in real and particular contexts, to achieve the goal of promoting "the progress of arts and science" or whether it is so irrevocably bound to print technologies that it no longer achieves its goals, or may actually work against them. Only with greater understanding of how the copyright system works in the real world can we use copyright law to make the information ecosystem sustainable. In complexity parlance, our aim should be to set legal rules that will help to keep the information ecosystem in a healthy, self-critical state, balancing stability against the elements of chaos that are essential to creativity.

Chapter 4
Chaos, Creativity, and Copyright

If the primary goal of copyright law is to encourage creativity by rewarding it, whether for reasons of moral entitlement or economic incentive, copyright law should contribute to the establishment of conditions that allow creativity to flourish. In complexity terms, it should set rules that are likely to produce sustainable creative systems. Complexity science suggests that the most robust complex adaptive systems exhibit self-organized criticality or positioning at the "edge of chaos." Their long-term sustainability hinges on their ability to maintain a state poised between order and disorder that allows them to adapt to changes in their environments. Sustainable systems follow rules that provide short-term stability, but also incorporate chaotic elements that permit emergence to occur. Scientific research to date indicates that this ability to balance, and profit from, both order and disorder may be a hallmark of human creativity.

This chapter considers the edge of chaos concept in relationship to creativity and the sustainability of the information ecosystem, beginning with what we know about creativity and its biological basis. The human brain, the organic seat of creativity, is generally recognized as one of the most complicated complex adaptive systems in our experience. With the help of new technologies, researchers are beginning to map its internal processes, overturning earlier theories about how the brain works. Research into the specific physiology underlying creativity is of relatively recent vintage. Nonetheless, what researchers have discovered thus far indicates that, like any successful complex adaptive system, the creative brain balances between stability and chaos; creativity emerges on that edge.

This chapter first reviews what we currently know about creativity and the brain. The argument then runs as follows. The creative process requires that the brain access elements of both order and chaos inherent in its own functioning. Copyright law may not directly touch the internal processes that produce creativity, but it does influence the environment in which the creative process occurs. It offers economic security to creators, but also controls the information available to the creative brain and the circumstances under which that information can be used. Copyright law itself has historically encompassed elements that both provide order and allow for some creative chaos, though it increasingly leans toward order. The complex nature of the creative process suggests that if copyright law is to encourage creativity, it must create an environment that both provides some stability for creators and accommodates a certain degree of churn.

Creativity Defined

With the arrival of digital technology, the study of creativity burgeoned, not only in neuroscience but also in fields like psychology and artificial intelligence. Researchers have attempted to define creativity, determine its physiological bases, map the creative process, and identify the environmental factors conducive to creativity. No universally accepted definition of "creativity" has emerged. Current definitions include:

1. The ability to combine novelty and usefulness in a particular social context;
2. The ability to restructure one's understanding of a situation in a nonobvious way;[1]
3. A combination of originality, utility, and creation of some product;[2]
4. The ability to come up with ideas that are new, surprising, and valuable.[3]

Like pornography, creativity is hard to define but we know it when we see it. There are two recurrent threads in these definitions: creativity involves something new (surprise, novelty, originality) but also has an element of usefulness (utility, value, product). The two threads often intertwine since novelty itself may impart value.

We might define humanity as the species that hates boredom. We value surprise and actively seek out the unpredictability it infuses into the quotidian. Moviegoers await the "twist" at the end of the film; art lovers seek out the latest "school;" fashion mavens model the newest trend. Recent research into the expressiveness of music suggests that the element of surprise, a subtle deviation from the musical pattern, is what elicits emotional response from the audience.[4] Creators and performers seek newness for themselves, but also recognize its value to their audiences. Apple designed the iPod with shuffle play because it understood the value music lovers placed on the unpredictable play list. Game makers incorporate alternative scenarios into videogames because players want variety in repeated plays. Yet the surprises we value are not always entirely random and neither is creativity.

---

1 Patricia Cohen, *Charting Creativity: Signposts of a Hazy Territory*, N.Y. TIMES, May 8, 2010, at C1.

2 NANCY C. ANDREASEN, THE CREATIVE BRAIN: THE SCIENCE OF GENIUS 17 – 18 (2005).

3 MARGARET A. BODEN, THE CREATIVE MIND: MYTHS AND MECHANISMS 1 (2d ed. 2004).

4 Pam Belluck, *To Tug at the Heart, Music First Must Tickle the Neurons*, N.Y. TIMES, Apr. 18, 2011, at D1.

Creativity surely involves open-ended play and exploration. It sometimes benefits from random or serendipitous occurrences. However, creative exploration is often guided by conceptual maps, kept within structural limits, and built on pre-existing knowledge. The shuffle play is confined to the music chosen by the listener. The video game software limits the action to certain characters and scenarios. Over time, creators use existing cultural elements as building blocks to create new cultural artifacts, gradually extending the reach of the creative arts and sciences.

As Europe emerged from the Dark Ages, Renaissance artists rediscovered classical perspective and proportion. Over several centuries, artists mapped the possibilities of realism, moving from the exquisite detail of Vermeer and Rembrandt, through the broken surfaces, bright palettes, and experimental perspectives of Impressionists and post-Impressionists, Expressionists, Symbolists, Fauves, and a variety of other movements. Finally, artists abandoned realism altogether, moving into pure abstraction, mapping out new visual space. In music, Bach systematically mapped the possibilities of the well-tempered tonal scale. Other composers over the centuries pushed tonality to its limits. Finally, twentieth-century composers abandoned tonality altogether, taking a further step in the mapping of musical space.[5]

In an early work on creativity and computation, Margaret Boden subdivided creativity into two types: (1) P-creativity—new and valuable to the particular creative person, but not new in history and (2) H-creativity—entirely new, never been thought of as far as we know in human history. The study of P-creativity can provide insights into the creative process, but H-creative ideas are more likely to drive progress in the arts and sciences. She further postulates three different ways in which creativity happens: (1) the creator develops unfamiliar combinations of familiar ideas; (2) a new idea unexpectedly fits into a pre-existing conceptual structure and allows new exploration of that conceptual space; (3) transformation: the new idea fits no existing conceptual structure, rather it is a game changer that entirely rewrites the conceptual road map. Analogies and metaphors, poetic imagery and collage, are examples of the first kind of creativity. New sonnets, new paintings in existing styles, new symphonies, exploration of the genetic components of evolution are examples of the second. Entirely new styles of art, such as cubism, entirely new theories of physics, such as general relativity or string theory, are examples of the third.[6] Thus, there are various levels of creativity. The

---

5 Boden, *supra* note 3, at 72–3.

6 *Id.*, at 2–6.

most creative people offer us new visions of the world we inhabit, but all levels of creativity contribute to culture and culture, in turn, provides the foundation for future creativity in a beneficial feedback loop that, if we are lucky, produces the progress of arts and science.

Creativity and the Brain

Researchers debate the distribution of creativity within the human populace. Some researchers distinguish between "ordinary" creativity, which is widely distributed and can be nourished through education, and "extraordinary" creativity possessed only by relatively rare, innately talented individuals.[7] Others suggest that creativity does not require some innate gift, but is simply an aspect of intelligence that exists in most people and may be enhanced by practice and the development of expertise.[8] All agree, however, that the brain is the primary organic seat of creativity. It is worth remembering that this recognition, in itself, is a relatively recent development in the history of the species. For most of human history, the brain remained a mystery because we lacked the technology to explore it, a difficulty perhaps compounded by the fact that the brain was both the object and the subject of the investigation.

The ancient Egyptians, in their efforts to ensure immortal life, mummified other organs of the body, but sucked the brain out of the skull and threw it away, believing that that heart was the locus of the soul. Aristotle thought the brain functioned essentially as an air conditioner for the blood, though Hippocrates favored the brain as the location for the soul. Descartes envisioned the brain as part of a hydraulic operation in which blood was transformed into animal spirits that were then dispensed throughout the body.[9] Not until the late 1880s did science possess the means to identify neurons or begin to associate certain neurological functions with different areas of the brain. Not until the mid twentieth century did technological advances enable the blossoming of neuroscience, and not until the development of technologies like functional magnetic resonance imaging (fMRI) were neuroscientists able to observe and map the activity of the brain at work and at "rest."

---

7 Andreasen, *supra* note 2, at 26–7.

8 Boden, *supra* note 3, at 35.

9 Nicholas Carr, The Shallows: What the Internet is Doing to our Brains 36–7 (2010).

The Brain as a Complex Adaptive System

Much of the brain is still terra incognita, but the work done thus far has revealed some surprising information about the brain and how it functions. While much is still unknown about the physiological basis of creativity, the information revealed by brain scans tends to correlate with macro-level research on creativity and with the stories told by creators themselves as reflected in qualitative analyses of creativity. Many brain scientists and creativity researchers approach the brain as a self-organizing complex adaptive system sharing the usual characteristics of such systems, including complicated structure, dynamism, nonlinearity, distributed control, and emergence.[10]

Even at a glance, the convoluted surfaces and bulging lobes of the brain display the characteristic intricate architecture of the complex adaptive system. Layers of nerve cells, the neurons, do the bulk of the brain's work. They form the outer surface, the "gray matter," of the brain. Each individual neuron extends out branches called dendrites, whose spines contain the synapses that connect neurons to each other. Neurons also send out longer connecting fibers, axons sheathed in myelin, which end in multiple synapses and form the white matter of the brain. Neurons communicate with each other by releasing chemical neurotransmitters that flow through the synapses and trigger or suppress electrical signals in the receiving neurons.[11]

Neurons are themselves complex adaptive systems nesting within the larger system of the brain.[12] There are well over a trillion neurons in the brain, making a literally incalculable number of synaptic connections, establishing neural circuits that contain both short and long feedback loops. The brain is, in other words, an enormously complex network. It is constantly active as it responds to innumerable external stimuli and the body's own internal requirements.[13] Like any complex system, it interacts extensively with its environment—not only the body it inhabits and controls, but also every environment through which that body moves, every tool it uses, every bit or byte of information it processes.

The brain imposes order on the mass of incoming data it processes, creating patterns that both constitute individual personality and make sense of the outside world. Ironically, the nonlinear, complex brain establishes linear, conscious

10 *See, e.g.*, Andreasen, *supra* note 2, at 61–3; Gyorgy Buzsaki, Rhythms of the Brain 10–15 (2006).

11 Andreasen, *id.*, at 52–61.

12 Buzsaki, *supra* note 10, at 11.

13 Andreasen, *supra* note 2, at 52–60.

thought processes that allow it to perform mental tasks; it assumes linear cause and effect relationships in the complex phenomena it observes. However, the brain also works at nonlinear, subconscious levels that brain scientists are only beginning to explore. While consciousness certainly arises from the brain, no single location within it seems to act as the "decider," the executive in charge of decision-making. Science has not yet discovered the neurological basis for consciousness, but some neuroscientists speculate that it may be an emergent phenomenon of the whole network, decentralized across the physical structures of the brain.[14] Two recent lines of discovery about the brain are particularly relevant to creativity: the neuroplasticity of the brain and the existence of the default mode.

Neuroplasticity

For many years, science described the brain as a static organ whose various parts were devoted to specific functions throughout life. Recent work has revealed that, to the contrary, the brain's structure is neuroplastic—it changes over time in response to experience, creating new neurons, carving new neural pathways, and abandoning old ones throughout life.[15] Some functions are associated with certain areas of the brain. The auditory and visual cortexes, for example, are specialized parts of the brain that hear sounds and receive visual stimuli. Nonetheless, the processing of such stimuli seems to involve many other areas of the brain. Language was once thought to be associated primarily with the left hemisphere of the brain; imaging studies have revealed that, in fact, language is processed in regions throughout the brain.[16]

The brain constantly reorganizes itself to respond to changes in its environment. In people who lose their sight or hearing, the brain compensates by building new neural connections that enhance hearing in the blind, visual acuity and other senses in the deaf.[17] The brain not only restructures itself in response to our life experiences, but also restructures in response to the physical and intellectual tools we use. The use of simple tools, like rakes or pliers or hammers, rewires the brain to perceive those tools as extensions of the hands.[18] Studies have shown that repetition of either physical or mental activities, such as playing a musical

[14] *Id.*, at 61–4.

[15] Barbara Strauch, The Secret Life of the Grown-up Brain: The Surprising Talents of the Middle-Aged Mind 59 (2010).

[16] Andreasen, *supra* note 2, at 64–6.

[17] Carr, *supra* note 9, at 29.

[18] *Id.*, at 32.

instrument or driving a cab in London, produce physical changes in areas of the brain that repeatedly process the same kind of information. The use of written language, and even of different alphabets, produces different brain circuitry than that found in nonliterate societies.[19]

Nicholas Carr compares the process of human intellectual maturation to the history of mapmaking. Children begin with simple, literal renderings of the landscape they see, without perspective or distance. As they mature, their drawings gradually incorporate knowledge of proportion and perspective, becoming increasingly realistic and dependent on calculation. Similarly, early maps were simple line drawings. Eventually, as human mental capabilities increased, maps became more realistic, capturing the proportions of the mapped space. Mapmakers came to rely on tools and mathematics to make more realistic maps. Finally maps were used to represent not only physical space, but also abstract ideas like forecasts of population growth. The more we used maps, the more they affected the way our brains perceived the world, allowing us to construct abstract, analogical spaces as well as to chart physical spaces.[20]

Neuroplasticity can have a down side. For good or ill, the neural pathways we use the most are carved the deepest and can be hardest to change. The brain is path dependent. Neural pathways that enhance musical performance may be desirable, but pathways that enhance depression, obsession, or addiction are not. Like emergent patterns in all complex adaptive systems, neural channels are indifferent to the quality or morality of the thought they enable. On the positive side of neuroplasticity: the longstanding assumption that the brain embarks on an inevitable downhill slide after age 20 has proven false. Recent studies show that while certain capacities, notably the ability to retrieve names and work at speed, decline with age, others are enhanced. The brain continues to add neurons, builds on experience, and utilizes more of its capacity as it ages, developing expertise or, more broadly, wisdom.[21]

These findings are relevant to the physical foundation of creativity in the brain. While much remains unknown or debated, previous assumptions about creativity have already been overturned. The common meme that creativity resides on the right side of the brain, rationality on the left appears to be incorrect. Creativity involves both hemispheres; it is not localizable to a certain area of the brain.[22] The

---

19 *Id.*, at 32–3, 51–2.

20 *Id.*, at 40–41.

21 Strauch, *supra* note 15, at 43–53.

22 Arne Dietrich, *Who's Afraid of a Cognitive Neuroscience of Creativity*, METHODS 42 (2007) at 25.

assumption that creativity dwindles with age also appears to be false. The brain as it ages accepts a broader range of inputs that may enhance creativity.[23] The neuroplastic nature of the brain, as studies have shown, assures that practice makes people more creative. Indeed, proponents of "embodied cognition" suggest that the body surrounding the brain makes its own contributions to cognitive activities.[24] While the brain is certainly at the center of cognition, the dancer's muscles, the painter's hands may also contribute to thought and, perhaps, creative inspiration. The more the artist works at painting, the writer at writing, the architect at design, the better and more creative she is likely to be. The creator's brain will accumulate more information about its field of endeavor, become more practiced in the art, and find new connections among the information it collects.

The Default Mode

The findings about the impact of neuroplasticity on creativity are complemented by recent studies concerning the brain's "default" mode. Brain scans have revealed continuous background activity, formerly considered to be mere noise, that goes on at a subconscious level when we are sleeping, or anaesthetized, or simply letting our minds wander. This default activity occurs throughout the brain as neurons fire in cycles coordinated by electrical signals. Each brain system has its own pattern of signaling, but signaling from some brain areas apparently takes precedence, imposing a degree of order on the chaos. The default mode network, with physical hubs in the middle of the brain, may be synchronizing the various parts of the brain, preparing it for the conscious activity which, we now know, forms only a small part of total brain activity.[25] Many decisions may actually be made at the subconscious level before they percolate into consciousness. The default mode may be central to consciousness; it may also be closely tied to creativity.

While research into the default mode is still very new, studies thus far indicate that the ability to access the default mode may produce the new linkages and insights that we associate with creativity — the "aha moment" in which a new insight presents itself. Some studies have shown that the brains of unusually creative people screen out fewer incoming perceptions than those of less creative people, who tend to discard much input unconsciously.[26] The ability to take in a

---

23 Strauch, *supra* note 15, at 89–90.

24 Andy Clark, *Out of our Brains*, N.Y.TIMES, OPINIONATOR, (Dec. 12, 2010: 3:47 PM), http://opinionator.blogs.nytimes.com/2010/12/12/out-of-our-brains/.

25 Marcus E. Raichle, *The Brain's Dark Energy,* SCI. AM., Mar. 2010, 44–9.

26 Andreasen, *supra* note 2, at 103–104.

broader set of inputs may foster creativity when combined with good executive skills to discriminate among ideas. Some brain scientists believe that without such skills, the same ability could foster mental illness; hence, the occasional association between creativity and some forms of mental illness, like bipolar disorder.[27] Some creative brains may tip over the edge into chaos.

The Creative Process

Creativity researchers have attempted to break down the creative process into steps. They have identified four basic stages: (1) preparation—collecting information, searching for related ideas, and listening to suggestions; (2) incubation—internal processing and organization of the material; (3) insight or illumination—the "Aha" moment, and (4) verification—evaluation of the insight and elaboration of it into its complete form.[28] A growing body of literature suggests that the process is not linear, but rather that chance, in one form or another, plays an important role in creativity. Neuroscientist Nancy Andreasen suggests that the creative process begins with disorganization as the brain "free associates" elements never previously linked, then gradually self-organizes to produce something completely new, whether it is a poem or a play or a software program. Others suggest that, at a minimum, creativity occurs when neurons essentially jump the track and fire randomly in novel patterns that are then incorporated into the brain's structure.[29]

In complexity terms, the brain contains elements of deterministic chaos, inherent in the complexity of its structure and processes, and elements of stability that, in a healthy brain, keep the chaos under control. Creativity may be an emergent property that occurs when the brain is poised at the edge of chaos, balanced between disorder and order, drawing on the subconscious as well as the conscious mind. As part of the creative process, the deterministic chaos inherent in the brain produces a new pattern that ultimately percolates into the conscious mind as an "aha moment" in which a new idea seems, to the creator, to come from nowhere. The creator then evaluates, formalizes, and elaborates on that insight.

This analysis of the way the brain works and the steps in the creative process seems to accord with observations of the work habits of creative people.

---

[27] *Id.*, at 101–107.

[28] Keith Sawyer, Explaining Creativity: The Science of Human Innovation 58–9 (2006).

[29] *See, e.g.*, Ralph D. Clifford, *Random Numbers, Chaos Theory, and Cogitation: A Search for the Minimal Creativity Standard in Copyright Law*, 82 Denv. U. L. Rev. 259, 274–9 (2004).

Notwithstanding the myth of the romantic artist as loner, most creative people collaborate with others in their fields and participate in social networks with other creative people. They collect and exchange information relevant to their creative areas. In fact, teams or industries produce many creative products, such as movies and videogames. Creative people often work within established forms, such as sonnets or software modules, and incorporate well-known subject matter into new matrices. Most creative people work hard at their craft, whatever it may be, spending long, structured hours honing their skills—building neural pathways. In other words, they prepare to be creative.

Yet most creative people also structure their work day to include idle time and report that "aha moments" most often occur during breaks from their current projects—while they are walking, reading, or working on an entirely different project or, in some cases, while they sleep.[30] Such insights may seem to come from nowhere, but often, in fact, the creator has done some preparation and her brain may have been subconsciously working on the project.[31] At least one study suggests that the unconscious default mode process will not engage with a problem until the conscious mind has defined the problem.[32]

Anecdotal descriptions of specific creative incidents by well-recognized creators also accord with the complexity framing of the creative process. J.K. Rowling is not alone among creators in reporting that inspiration for a major work appeared, seemingly unbidden, in her mind. Coleridge famously dreamed the poem *Kubla Khan* while sleeping under the influence of a drug, possibly opium, prescribed for ill health. He had been reading a description of Kubla Khan's palace, composed the lines of the poem in a dream state, and, upon awakening, wrote down as many of the lines as he could recall. The poem remains unfinished as a consequence of an interruption by a visitor, after which Coleridge could no longer recall the remaining lines he had dreamed.[33] Friedrich von Kekule puzzled over the structure of the benzene molecule for years. One day while dozing in front of the fire, he envisioned strings of atoms twisting like snakes, one of which seized its own tail. He awoke knowing that the structure of benzene was a ring, and founded a new branch of chemistry.[34] Many creators have reported incidents in which new works, whether entire musical compositions or mathematical

30 Sawyer, *supra* note 28, at 62.

31 Boden, *supra* note 3, at 26–9.

32 Carr, *supra* note 9, at 119.

33 Andreasen, *supra* note 2, at 19–22.

34 Boden, *supra* note 3, at 25–8.

formulae, arose fully-fledged from the subconscious, to be consciously formalized and elaborated.[35]

Other creators report slipping into states of intense concentration divorced from reality, writing without conscious direction, or generally letting the mind wander while in the creative state, collecting input from the external world and allowing the mind to make whatever unexpected connections it will. Such accounts jibe with the notion of a complex adaptive brain taking advantage of chaotic elements, redirecting neural pathways, then building new architecture along those pathways. Creators benefit from the chaotic elements that produce new insights, but they also incorporate those insights into new structures, just as the brain, despite its own deterministic chaos, imposes patterns that control our perceptions of the world around us.

Recent studies on moviemaking and viewing reveal an interesting relationship between the physical brain and this category of creative works. One study suggests that the structure of shots in movies—the bundling of different lengths of film segments from scene to scene—has evolved over the years to resemble a wave pattern called "pink noise" which is widely distributed throughout the natural world and in the rhythms of the brain itself. Pink noise has a signal profile that is neither completely random nor completely ordered; it exists at the edge of chaos. The underlying frequencies of images, the human heartbeat, the tides, traffic, or stock market movements, all graph as pink noise. So does the reaction time of the brain as we focus and refocus our attention. The study indicates that recent movies come much closer to approximating that same pattern than did movies 50 years ago. Consequently, the shot rhythms of newer movies force us to focus more on the movie than they formerly did.[36] The creative brains of directors may be, if only subconsciously, synchronizing films to self-critical frequencies.

As to movie audiences, a study of film watchers found that adults watching the same film exhibited the same pattern of brain activity, activating the same areas of the brain in unison. They also exhibited repressed activity in the prefrontal cortex, associated with self-awareness, allowing the viewers to lose themselves in the film. Sensory inputs were heightened, self-awareness inhibited. Their brains synchronized when exposed to the same visual input.[37] Brain scans of speakers

---

[35] Andreasen, *supra* note 2, at 36–45.

[36] Natalie Angier, *Bringing New Understanding to the Director's Cut*, N.Y.TIMES, Mar. 1, 2010, at D1.

[37] Jonah Lehrer, *The Neuroscience of Inception*, WIRED.COM, WIRED SCIENCE, THE FRONTAL CORTEX (Jul. 26, 2010, 12:41 PM), http://www.wired.com/wiredscience/2010/07/the-neuroscience-of-inception/.

and listeners during storytelling have also shown such synchronicity.[38] Perhaps creators' brains, marching to their own internal rhythms, inherently seek to create patterns that match the natural rhythms of their audiences' brains. There may be a physiological basis not only for creativity, but also for appreciation of creative works.

The Creative Environment

Nurture is as important to the development of the brain and to creativity as basic physiology. Some of the architecture of the brain is genetically determined, but the brain reshapes itself throughout life. Creative people may have innate abilities, but their use of them will be encouraged or discouraged by the environment in which they live. In fact, clusters of particularly creative periods and places appear throughout human history: Athens in the fourth and fifth centuries BCE; Florence during the Renaissance; England under the Tudors or during the Romantic Era; France during the Enlightenment; the United States at its founding in the late 1700s or at any time during the twentieth century explosion of new media and new art. Creative work is certainly done outside of these periods, but certain social, political, and economic conditions maximize creativity. The creative brain, like all complex adaptive systems, interacts with other complex adaptive systems and responds to its environment.

Andreasen suggests that "cradles of creativity" share certain characteristics: intellectual freedom—a ferment of cutting-edge ideas; a critical mass of creative people who exchange such ideas—a social network; fair competition among creators; a system of mentors and patrons, and economic prosperity. The first four assure that the creative brain communicates with other creative brains, both living and dead, through shared culture. The fifth enables the other four by, among other things, allowing the accumulation of intellectual resources that creators can build on, such as libraries, museums, or, nowadays, the Internet. It also assures that creators have the financial resources to pay for their materials and that patrons have the wherewithal to pay for the resulting works.[39] These conditions mix order (prosperity, mentors, patrons) with chaos (intellectual ferment, idea exchange, intense but fair competition). They produce an environment in which creators' lives are stable enough to give them the time, place, and means to create, but

---

[38] Brandon Keim, *Good Connection Really Does Lead to Mind Meld*, WIRED. COM, WIRED SCIENCE (Jul. 26, 2010, 3:00 PM), http://www.wired.com/wiredscience/2010/07/mind-meshing/.

[39] Andreasen, *supra* note 2, at 127–32.

also the opportunity to experiment, push the boundaries of received wisdom, or develop entirely new conceptual maps. In short, creative environments are those that encourage creative people to push toward the edge of chaos where creativity lies.

Both the human brain and conceptions of creativity continue to evolve. New electronic technologies may be rewiring our brains and certainly pose challenges to our pre-existing definitions of creativity. If, as studies have shown, the use of physical or intellectual tools reshapes the physiology of the brain, what might be the effects of our constant interaction with the dominant tools of the present age, networked computing devices? A debate currently rages about the impact of digital media on the brain. Critics of Internet culture, supported by some scientific studies, suggest that our brains are adapting to the ever-present global network by losing the ability to concentrate and reflect. Electronic media encourage users to skip down a chain of hyperlinks from one bit of information to the next, skimming along the surface, never pausing to consolidate or analyze the information being absorbed. Recent research suggests that our use of digital technology may hamper our ability to consolidate information in long-term memory, an essential aspect of intelligence and creativity.[40]

Short-term working memory holds our immediate consciousness, the perceptions of the moment. Long-term memory files information away for future use, but also organizes it into concepts or "schema" which form the basis for understanding, but remain unconscious until the information is brought back into working memory. While long-term memory has vast capacity, working memory can hold only a small quantity of information at one time, creating a bottleneck in information flow, or "cognitive load," within the brain. It takes time for working memory to transfer information into long-term memory. Where analog information sources, like books, provided a slow, steady transfer of coherent information into long-term memory, electronic media blast vast amounts of disconnected information into short-term memory, only bits of which make the jump to long-term memory.[41] Citing recent scientific studies, Nicholas Carr suggests that, in the face of this fire hose flow of information, our brains lose the ability to consolidate information, concentrate, and think deeply, with adverse effects on creativity.[42] Carr bemoans the loss of linear thought encouraged by the printed book and the rise of constant distraction encouraged by the Internet.

---

40 Carr, *supra* note 9, at 182–97.

41 *Id.*, at 123–5.

42 *Id.*, at 191–5.

Others, adopting the language of complexity, embrace the abandonment of linear thinking, discovering emergent meaning in constantly changing contexts.[43] Proponents of Internet culture observe that it enables entirely new forms of individual and collective creativity, engaging more people than ever before in creative enterprises.[44] They celebrate, for example, the "crowdsourcing" of problem-solving tasks to communities of people, a technique that has successfully solved complex mathematical equations and created comprehensive databases of information on a variety of topics. They tout the development of online resources like Wikipedia, the encyclopedia produced by volunteers. For these observers, the broadening of cultural engagement is an acceptable trade-off for the deeper, but narrower, creativity of the printed book. Connectivity may be an essential element of creativity. Thus, our very definition of creativity could change in the new digital environment.

Copyright Law and Creativity

Whether digital technologies enhance creativity or handicap it, copyright law will clearly play a role in setting the parameters of digital creativity. While laws do not directly touch the internal workings of the creative brain, they certainly affect the environment in which it lives and the information available for it to work with. Copyright's purported goal is to create a climate conducive to creativity by providing economic security for creators, one of the foundational elements for cradles of creativity. It creates economic incentives to replace the old patronage system. It intends, in other words, to provide the nurture needed to enhance the creative nature. Yet it also, at least in theory, should encourage intellectual freedom and the exchange of ideas by protecting the public domain. If it is to lay the groundwork for a sustainable creative environment, it must nudge creators, and the copyright systems that support them, toward the edge of chaos yet prevent them from falling over it.

Moreover, if the purpose of copyright is to encourage creativity, it seems evident that copyright law itself may have to change if our mode of creativity changes. If our brains are indeed being rewired for different creative modes, we must question whether the basic precepts of copyright law can make the transition to an electronic information ecosystem or are too inflexibly tied to analog

---

43 *Id.*, at 111.

44 Clay Shirky, Cognitive Surplus: Creativity and Generosity in a Connected Age 12–29 (2010).

technologies and creative forms to survive. If the essence of creativity involves a balancing act between chaos and order, we must determine whether copyright law contributes to that creative equipoise or tips so much toward order that it actively hampers new forms of creativity.

Our first inquiry should be whether current copyright law acknowledges or incorporates the concepts of creativity just discussed. The larger inquiry is whether it creates an environment conducive to creativity. Certainly, copyright law is no stranger to the concept of balancing interests, though the process is seldom phrased in terms of balancing order and disorder. In the utilitarian view, copyright law explicitly seeks to balance private gain against public access. Even civil law regimes balance the creator's moral rights in his works against the requirements of economic exploitation. In creating monopolies, copyright attempts to provide economic stability for creators. Yet, in theory, copyright limits those monopolies to protect the public domain in order to make available the cultural building blocks necessary for experimentation, competition, and intellectual freedom—the chaotic elements essential to creativity.

Copyright offers some protection for both works that are useful and those that are novel or surprising. Early copyright laws concentrated most on the useful, as the U.S. constitutional phrasing "the progress of science and useful arts" implies. The earliest copyright acts protected only books, maps, and charts, a focus clearly derived from their intention to control the specific medium of print publishing. Books cover a broad range from the useful to the entirely fanciful. Maps, on the other hand, must hew closely to the facts of topography and geography if they are to be useful. The creative is here the enemy of the true. Yet maps were among the first subject matters of copyright because of their usefulness.

At copyright's birth, Western civilizations were still charting both the oceans and large continents like the Americas—maps and charts were both indispensable and costly to create so copyright encouraged their making with a limited monopoly. Only later did copyright expand to include expression, like the traditional fine arts, that is predominantly creative, but not necessarily "useful" in the usual sense of that word. Copyright law now admits to protection many works on a broad spectrum from the highly creative, such as paintings or sculpture, to works such as compilations of data or collective works that, on their faces, possess little creativity, but are quite useful. It ecumenically protects both the useful and the surprising or new, but does not necessarily require that a work possess both qualities. The originality requirement, as constrained by limitations protecting the public domain, sets the creativity threshold for copyright protection.

The Originality Requirement

"Originality" is globally required for copyright protection and is meant to relegate unoriginal works to the public domain. The content of the originality requirement varies from country to country. Common law countries historically required little more than independent creation or the infusion of skill or labor, while many European countries required a higher degree of creativity in accordance with the moral rights tradition of the civil law. Some common law countries have recently moved closer to the European model under the influence of international treaties. The Berne Convention and TRIPs require their signatories to harmonize their originality requirements to a certain minimum. That process has faced some path resistance because of the variations in interpretation under different national copyright laws.[45] The originality requirement is not necessarily contiguous with creativity in the broad sense used by creativity researchers both because of varying interpretations and because of the necessity of balancing economic incentives against access for users and follow-on creators.

In the United States, mere independent creation met the originality requirement for almost two centuries under case law that focused quite literally on whether the copyright owner "originated" the work or merely copied it. Courts explicitly rejected "novelty" or uniqueness as a requirement for copyright protection.[46] They declined to make judgments about levels of creativity or the worthiness of copyrighted works.[47] Prior to the Supreme Court decision to the contrary in *Feist Publications, Inc. v. Rural Telephone Service Co.*,[48] a number of lower courts had granted copyright protection to useful compilations like catalogs and directories because of the labor, "the sweat of the brow," invested in them, even in the absence of any hint of originality.[49] Originality so interpreted bears a strong relationship to usefulness, but less relationship to the qualities of newness or surprise that characterize creativity in the broader sense. *Feist* altered the content of the originality requirement. In a strongly utilitarian opinion, the Court found that the Constitution required some minimal level of creativity for copyright protection, a minimum not met by the traditional white pages of a telephone directory. The

---

[45] *See*, MARY LAFRANCE, GLOBAL ISSUES IN COPYRIGHT LAW 24–37 (2009).

[46] Alfred Bell & Co. v. Catalda Fine Arts, 191 F.2d 99, 102 (2d Cir. 1951).

[47] Bleistein v. Donaldson Lithographing Co., 188 U.S. 239, 251–2 (1903).

[48] 499 U.S. 340 (1991).

[49] *See, e.g.*, Leon v. Pacific Telephone & Telegraph Co., 91 F.2d 484 (9th Cir. 1937) (telephone directory copyrightable); Jeweler's Circular Publishing Co. v. Keystone Publishing Co., 281 F. 83 (2d Cir. 1922) (directory of jewelers copyrightable).

court gave little guidance as to what that level might be, though it did indicate that the standard was relatively low. In so doing, it inserted a creativity requirement beyond mere usefulness, and certainly challenged lower courts to define the creative minimum in the circumstances of subsequent cases, with predictably unpredictable results.

As the scope of copyright expanded, the content of the originality requirement was tested by new technologies as well as by the inclusion of works that involved sweat equity but lacked "creativity" in the traditional sense. Photography, for example, does not require the manual skills of painting or sculpture, but Congress brought it within the scope of copyright and the courts found originality in the decisions made before the snap of the shutter: choice of subject, pose, lighting, background, camera angle. The addition of software to the catalog of protected works created challenges for the originality requirement given developers' common practice of sharing and reusing software modules and the standardized requirements for machine interoperability. In the EU, which adopted a Computer Program Directive[50] to harmonize the law among member states, those challenges were often met by tinkering with the originality requirement to require a somewhat lower standard of creativity for software than for other works.[51] In the United States, courts instead manipulated doctrines associated with the idea/expression dichotomy to winnow out unprotectable aspects of computer programs, leaving commonly used programming modules, interfaces essential for machine interoperability, and the like, available for use by other programmers.[52]

By and large, works meeting the originality threshold get full protection under a one-size-fits-all system. But, in some instances, as with software, copyright law recognizes and compensates for lower levels of creativity by providing somewhat lower levels of protection. Compilers of factual works like telephone directories, or collective works like anthologies, receive protection only for their selection and arrangement of materials and any new material they add. As the *Feist* court noted, even selection and arrangement receive only "thin" protection, that is, they can only be infringed by near identical copying. Creators of works derived from the copyrightable works of others receive protection only for the new material they themselves create. Musical compositions and lyrics achieved copyright protection long before the sound recordings that often embody particular performances of

---

[50] Council Directive 2009/24/EC, adopted Apr. 23, 2009, reproduced in Michel M. Walter and Silke Von Lewinski, European Copyright Law: A Commentary 88–9 (2010).

[51] *Id.*, at 93–8.

[52] Computer Associates International, Inc., v. Altai, Inc., 982 F.2d. 693, 706–8 (2nd Cir. 1992).

such works. When Congress added sound recordings to the ranks of the copyright-protected, it granted a rather more restricted bundle of rights, excluding the public performance[53] and display rights granted to other categories of copyrighted works, and limiting the reproduction right to literal copying.

Copyright's originality requirement is sufficiently generous to protect both P-creativity (new to the person) and H-creativity (new to history). A P-creative work may receive copyright protection as long as it is independently created, rather than copied, even though it is not entirely novel. H-creative works may similarly receive protection at least with regard to their expression. In both kinds of works, protection may be withheld from the ideas and facts contained therein or may be limited by doctrines like fair use. Similarly, the author's expression is protectable whether the author develops unfamiliar combinations of familiar ideas, works a new idea into a pre-existing conceptual structure and explores the reconfigured conceptual space, or expounds on a transformative new idea that fits no existing conceptual structure. The limiting doctrines of copyright, however, also come into play to reserve certain building block ideas for the public domain, make them accessible to creators, or allow fair uses under appropriate circumstances, thereby enabling the intellectual ferment and idea exchange that contributes to creativity.

Limiting Doctrines

Law's most basic function is to provide predictable rules for societal interaction. It is an inherently conservative discipline and copyright, like most laws, leans toward order. Law can, of course, inadvertently create disorder where it is poorly formulated or where it is repeatedly amended without attention to its overarching purpose or framework. Judicial interpretation may step in to smooth over such anomalies. Copyright law contains a number of bright line rules, such as the rules governing formalities, setting scope and duration, or setting penalties, which are conducive to predictable behaviors. Historically, however, courts have often initiated limiting doctrines that provide copyright with the flexibility to adapt to novel situations as they arise.

These doctrines often take the form of so-called "muddy" rules. A rule is muddy if the outcome of its application to an entitlement dispute is unpredictable and requires the decision maker to balance competing interests. A degree of muddiness is inherent in statutory language that requires judicial interpretation—terms such as "originality," "fixation," or "copy"—as well as in the complicated,

---

[53] Congress later granted a public performance right in digital audio transmissions to cover Internet streaming of sound recordings. 17 U.S.C. § 106(6).

multifactored test for copyright infringement. Additionally, limiting doctrines like fair use and the idea/expression dichotomy exemplify muddy rules that leave courts with a good deal of discretion to tweak the law as it applies to particular situations. In the United States, these limiting doctrines were later incorporated into actual statutory text, though they retain their characteristics as "muddy" rules designed to provide courts with discretion in the application of the law to particular facts. While muddy rules provide the flexibility necessary to sustain the doctrinal system, allowing it to adapt to changing circumstances, they also introduce considerable unpredictability into the system. Historically, they have played a significant role in preventing copyright owners from achieving complete control over every use of copyrighted works, leaving materials available to users and later creators.

The idea/expression dichotomy is one of several doctrines created by American courts to limit the reach of copyright protection even as legislators continuously added new categories of works to copyright's ambit. Originally formulated in *Baker v. Selden*[54] and now codified,[55] the doctrine provides that copyright protection shall not extend to ideas, procedures, processes, systems, methods of operation, concepts, principles, or discoveries. The related doctrine of merger provides that protection does not extend to the expression of ideas that can only be expressed in one or a limited number of ways. Similarly, the doctrine of "scenes a faire" excludes from protection characters, plot points, or settings that are standard in treatment of a given topic: for example, scenes of beer halls and "Heil Hitler" salutes in stories dealing with Nazi Germany.

The dichotomy has been incorporated into Article 2 of the WIPO Copyright Treaty,[56] Article 9.2 of TRIPs,[57] and Article 1.2 of the EU Computer Program Directive,[58] which may broaden its impact outside of the United States. The doctrine draws a line between the copyright and patent regimes, but also sets aside valuable terrain in the public domain from which creators will be permitted to build new works. It channels ideas, no matter how creative, into the public domain and functional methods and processes into the patent regime. Its application

---

54 101 U.S. 99 (1879).

55 17 U.S.C. § 102(b) (2006).

56 WIPO.INT, WIPO Copyright Treaty, Art. 2, Dec. 20, 1996, *available at* http://www.wipo.int/treaties/en/ip/wct/trtdocs_wo033.html#P87_12240.

57 WTO.ORG, *TRIPs: Text of the Agreement*, Apr. 15, 1994, Art. 9.2, *available at* http://www.wto.org/english/tratop_e/trips_e/t_agm0_e.htm.

58 Walter and Von Lewinski, *supra* note 50.

requires courts to make difficult, highly discretionary judgments dividing ideas from expression in particular works.

Another such court-created doctrine, the first sale doctrine,[59] limits the copyright owner's right of distribution to its original sale of a legitimate copy, after which the buyer can freely redistribute the copy. In the United States, the first sale doctrine enables the secondary market in used books and the formation of public libraries, significantly increasing public access to creative works and providing the cultural resources essential for future creators. The doctrine is not, however, accepted in the EU. Many civil law countries provide authors with a right to royalties on both resale and public lending of copies. Where it does exist, the doctrine provides a freedom to users of analog works that is rapidly vanishing in electronic contexts. In digital media, redistribution typically involves the making of a perfect copy, thereby simultaneously violating the reproduction right under prevailing judicial interpretations of copying and fixation. Software developers, in particular, have successfully used licensing agreements to nullify buyers' ability to redistribute their works, a practice that a few academic publishers have sought to emulate even in hard copy works. Legislative attempts to formulate an electronic equivalent of the first sale doctrine have failed thus far.

Fair use, or fair dealing, is perhaps the broadest of the court-created doctrines limiting copyright protection. The doctrine evolved from a doctrine of fair abridgement originated by the English Chancery Courts.[60] In the United States, the doctrine was first formulated by the Supreme Court in *Folsom v. Marsh*,[61] and elaborated upon in subsequent decisions. Now codified,[62] fair use provides an affirmative defense to unauthorized users of copyrighted materials where such use serves beneficial public purposes such as education, critical commentary, or news reporting. The doctrine establishes four nonexclusive factors that courts must consider in fair use cases: the purpose and character of the defendant's use; the nature of the copyrighted work; the amount and substantiality of the material taken from the copyrighted work, and the effect upon the copyright owner's markets. Each of the four factors now incorporates a number of further inquiries.

Not surprisingly under such a complicated, multifactored test, the precise scope of the doctrine is hellishly difficult to predict and closely tied to the facts of particular cases. Yet, of all the limitations on copyright, it is perhaps the

---

59 In the United States, the Supreme Court created the doctrine in Bobbs-Merrill Co. v. Straus, 210 U.S. 339 (1908). It is now codified as 17 U.S.C. § 109(a) (2006).

60 Gyles v Wilcox, 26 ER 489 (1740).

61 Folsom v. Marsh, 9 F.Cas. 342 (1841).

62 17 U.S.C. § 107 (2006).

most closely related to the qualities of newness and surprise often cited as the hallmarks of creativity. American courts have used fair use, in conjunction with other doctrines, to protect technological innovations like videotape recorders[63] and reverse-engineered software.[64] They now consider the "transformativeness" of the defendant's work under the first factor of fair use doctrine, offering fair use more freely to highly transformative works. Thus far, the transformativeness analysis has prevented copyright owners from blocking the creation and use of works as diverse as parodies[65] and search engine technologies.[66] Such applications map well onto traditional conceptions of creativity.

On the other hand, in recent years, the courts have resisted fair use claims for literal copying technologies like file sharing software, handily shutting down peer-to-peer file sharing sites without regard to claims that such sharing actually enhanced sales or that the services were also used to share noninfringing materials.[67] The DMCA, while paying lip service to fair use, provides no general fair use exception, limiting the concept to very specific exceptions established by the Librarian of Congress during triennial reviews. Moreover, judicial limitations crafted on a case-by-case basis after lengthy, expensive court battles must be read against a backdrop of continuous legislative expansion of the duration and scope of copyright.

Durational limits were originally the chief tactic for balancing the interests of creators against the interests of the public and of future creators, keeping copyright monopolies within bounds. The series of term extensions that national legislatures have adopted and then promulgated through treaty keep a broad variety of creative works out of the public domain, and thus out of the hands of follow-on creators, for a much longer time than that envisioned by copyright's creators. That extended duration is matched by vastly expanded scope. Copyright law's path has clearly been in the direction of broader and longer monopolies that, by their very nature, have the potential to inhibit the free competition and exchange of ideas important to highly creative periods.

---

63 Sony Corp. of America v. Universal City Studios, Inc. 464 U.S. 417 (1984).

64 Sega Enterprises, Ltd. v. Accolade, Inc., 977 F.2d 1510 (9th Cir. 1992).

65 Campbell v. Acuff-Rose Music, Inc., 510 U.S. 569 (1994).

66 Perfect 10, Inc. v. Amazon.com, Inc., 508 F.3d 1146 (9th Cir. 2007).

67 *See, e.g.*, A & M Records, Inc. v. Napster, Inc. 239 F.3d 1004 (9th Cir. 2001); Metro-Goldwyn-Mayer Studios, Inc. v. Grokster, Ltd. 545 U.S. 913 (2005).

Copyright and the Creative Environment

On the whole, then, the copyright regime, while it might not closely track current concepts of creativity in all respects, does encompass elements of order and disorder that might be conducive to creativity if appropriately balanced. It incorporates requirements for minimal creativity and even occasionally calibrates the level of protection for different levels of creativity. It has come to embody both bright line rules and a set of "muddy" rules that, taken together, provide stability and flexibility, predictability leavened by surprise. While we have little empirical proof of its effectiveness, copyright law does seem to recognize many of the basic requirements for creative environments. Over several centuries, copyright's limiting doctrines have offered protection for the free exchange of ideas, intellectual ferment, and fair competition characteristic of such environments. Nonetheless, copyright law has become increasingly less receptive to the disorder that accompanies creativity, particularly as legislatures have responded to recent threats posed to influential copyright industries by electronic media. Of course, copyright law constitutes only one set of rules for copyright systems. The forces of creative disorder spring from other sources outside of, and increasingly in conflict with, copyright law.

Copyright law has, for much of its history, cooperated with social norms and market practices to provide a relatively orderly structure for the creation, licensing, and distribution of creative works within its scope without unduly restricting creative activity. The relative flexibility of copyright law, abetted by technological inability to track all uses of works, permitted a variety of creative re-uses of cultural materials that essentially flew below copyright's radar. Personal and shared uses of copyrighted materials by individual consumers, while often merely consumptive, also included adaptive and creative uses of works. These activities provided training grounds for the next generation of musicians or writers without economic effect on the copyright owner and, as in the case of mere consumptive sharing, often without its knowledge. If a Star Trek fan remodeled his family room to emulate the deck of the Enterprise, no significant harm was done to Paramount, the owner of the space opera franchise. Paramount was unlikely even to discover the copying, at least until the documentary *Trekkies* was released.

As with consumptive copying, when such derivative works existed only in analog forms, they posed little commercial threat to copyright owners who grudgingly tolerated them because they built the product's fan base. Digitization materially altered the rules of the game. Users not only achieved the ability to make perfect copies, they also acquired the ability to modify that content in ways that might take the authors' original conceptions in entirely new and different directions, some of which might harm the copyright owner's markets. When a fan now reproduces the Enterprise in virtual space and shares it not merely with family and close friends, but with a global network of electronic "acquaintances," his creative "enterprise" may impinge on Paramount's own commercial uses in cyberspace. When he writes fan fiction that uses Spock or Captain Kirk in new storylines, he may develop the characters in ways not foreseen or approved of by the copyright owner. Copyright owners have taken the warpath not only against copying but also against various forms of creative re-use, seeking stronger legal protections and using increasingly advanced technological systems to track every use of every work and punish every infringement.

The recent trend in legislation and in treaty negotiation favors enhanced control by copyright owners. Such control is not merely aimed at eliminating consumptive copying; it also targets many creative re-uses of copyrighted materials and, in doing so, would eliminate much creative activity that was allowed in the analog world. Courts also appear increasingly reluctant to impose muddy limitations on legislatures' decided embrace of strong protection. Indeed, the use of muddy rules as tools of flexibility becomes more problematic generally as the law now targets ordinary users, living their lives without benefit of counsel, rather than business competitors. Copyright's natural tendency toward order may be taking on a decided slant toward rigidity, fencing off increasingly larger cultural acreage.

The trend toward owner control is exemplified in the recent, ongoing legal dispute over the Google digital library project. Google, in collaboration with a number of respected libraries, inaugurated a project designed to scan every book ever published, whether in copyright or in the public domain, and make them all available in electronic form—a digital re-creation, on an enormous scale, of the ancient Library of Alexandria that contained all the knowledge of the (then) known world. On the face of it, the library offered many benefits: enhanced access to a huge repository of information, facilitation of conversion of books to formats accessible by the handicapped, preservation of works, even new audiences for copyright owners. The details of Google's tracking and control of the information raised concerns among many observers about electronic monopoly and invasion of privacy. However, the chief concern of the Association of American Publishers and the Authors Guild of America, both of which immediately sued Google, was copyright infringement. They claimed that Google's scanning plan was an exercise in massive infringement of their members' rights in works still protected by copyright. Google claimed fair use, but the parties ultimately negotiated a proposed settlement, that would have imposed a pay-per-use system on any digitized books that were still in copyright.[68] Snippets of copyrighted books would have been freely available, but entire books would have only been accessible to those who could afford to pay. So much for the Library of Alexandria!

The court rejected the proposed settlement, expressing its discomfort with the fact that the settlement might implement a forward-looking business arrangement that would reward Google, and only Google, with rights to exploit books without copyright owners' permission and give it significant advantages over any competitors. The court was particularly concerned that the settlement would create a de facto monopoly over orphan books—copyrighted books whose copyright holders cannot be identified or found. Moreover, the plaintiffs did not represent large numbers of copyright holders, such as academic authors, and foreign authors would be put at a distinct disadvantage in determining whether their rights were affected by the settlement. The court left open the possibility that the parties might rewrite the settlement, but the future direction of the lawsuit remains unknown as of this writing.[69]

If the settlement had prevailed, the digital library of the future would bear little resemblance to the physical library of today, where potential creators may browse at will through both public domain and copyrighted works, giving the creative brain free access to a wealth of cultural information and the opportunity to carve out new neural pathways and build new creations. Instead of the digital, democratic recreation of the Alexandrian library originally envisioned for the project, a goodly portion of humanity's written heritage would be locked behind digital gates, accessible only to those able to pay. Noncommercial models for publicly supported digital libraries are underway in other countries, including France, the Netherlands, Australia, Finland, and Norway. Similar proposals have been made in the United States, but require private funding and would probably exclude works still in copyright unless the rights holders agreed to their use.[70] Even noncommercial proposals in the U.S. appear likely to be more limited in content than the analog public library.

The intellectual ferment and free exchange of ideas that produce cradles of creativity are not likely to be promoted by locking cultural resources behind pay-per-use gates or excluding them from digital use. As long as analog copies of

---

68 Google Book Settlement, *Amended Settlement Agreement*, at http://www.googlebooksettlement.com/agreement.html (last visited May 11, 2011).

69 The Authors Guild v. Google, Inc., 05 CIV.8136 (DC), 2011 WL 986049 (S.D.N.Y. Mar. 22, 2011).

70 Robert Darnton, *A Digital Library Better than Google's*, N.Y. Times, Mar. 23, 2011, at A31.

works are available in real world libraries, those resources can be used, if less conveniently. But libraries themselves are increasingly replacing analog works with digital versions to which copyright holders attach restrictions never previously imposed on analog copies of works.[71] Certainly, copyright industries have reason to feel threatened by the new electronic environment. Some of them may ultimately go the way of player piano roll manufacturers. Others will adapt and survive. There is a danger that, in their struggle to preserve their current business models, they will influence legislatures to enact overly muscular copyright laws that may actually reduce the sustainability of the creative enterprise, pushing it away from the edge of chaos and frustrating the original purpose of copyright law. Stringent laws and enforcement may inhibit creativity by preventing the chaotic reuse, reimagining, and remixing of cultural materials. New creators may be deprived of the building blocks they need to produce new works; the public may be deprived of free access to works that contribute to the common culture.

In the last 20 years, ordinary people have latched on to new digital tools and used them to produce their own works, both original and derivative. Digital technologies combined with the increased free time of educated citizens—what Clay Shirky refers to as "cognitive surplus"[72]—have produced terabytes of new information from nonprofessional creators who now have the means to create and the ability to communicate their creations globally. Every weekend photographer or videographer can create, edit, enhance, and disseminate works of near professional quality. Every would-be writer can seek an audience on the Internet. Formerly passive users have become active creators. Many of their works build, without permission, on copyrighted works. For every song or video clip copied merely to avoid payment, there are also many user-creators building new works on existing materials, sending novel memes ricocheting through the cultural network. A straightforward movie scene of Hitler confronting his generals generates hundreds of resubtitled parodies on the latest issues in politics, technology, and popular culture. Popular franchises like Harry Potter or Star Wars spin off thousands of fan-created stories, mini-movies (some performed by Legos), and virtual environments. Whether such works are shallow or deep, fine art or foolishness, they are certainly creative and, for better or worse, they are reshaping our common culture and rewiring our brains.

---

[71] Cory Doctorow, *HarperCollins to Libraries: We Will Nuke Your E-books after 26 Checkouts*, BoingBoing (Feb. 25, 2011, 12:41 PM), http://boingboing.net/2011/02/25/harpercollins-to-lib.html.

[72] Shirky, *supra* note 44, at 9.

On the Edge of Chaos

It may be that copyright law, no matter how strictly enforced, cannot completely rein in this wave of technology-enabled creative activity. Strongly worded laws with heavier penalties may hamper user creativity by impeding access to cultural materials, though efforts to date have not produced impressive results. What such measures have done quite effectively is breed contempt for copyright law itself and for the major industries that profit from it. While rampant sharing certainly threatens existing copyright owners, rigid propertization of their rights may threaten copyright itself as a conceptual complex adaptive system that, like any such system, must be poised on the edge of chaos if it is to be sustainable.

Chaotic elements—the random fires on prairies, creative destruction in economies—are essential to complex adaptive systems. Copyright owners who attempt to control every use of every work effectively seek a new Stationers' monopoly, expanded to include new digital media and functioning as an instrument of censorship not by governments but by corporations. Such abandonment of the historic principles of copyright law presents two perils. The first is that it leaves no room for the experimentation essential to creativity and, consequently, discourages creation rather than incentivizing it. The second is that users may dismiss copyright as hopelessly outdated, route around it, and, in so doing, destroy any economic safety net that it provides for creators. Copyright law could become the USSR of the twenty-first century—a system so heavily structured that it lacks the flexibility to evolve in response to a rapidly changing world. If copyright law cannot adapt to new technologies and emergent social and creative networks, the system itself may reach a tipping point beyond which it becomes unsustainable.

In the analog world, copyright law acted much like the membrane of a cell. It provided a protected environment for creators and copyright industries, keeping them afloat economically. It was also, however, permeable and elastic, allowing considerable information to flow out to the shared culture where it fostered new creations that subsequently flowed back into copyright's ambit. For copyright law itself to remain viable, it may have to recognize and reclaim this permeability. Rather than embarking on a legal effort to plug every possible leak by giving copyright owners complete control over their works, we should try to locate the critical pressure points where order must be maintained or creative chaos permitted to flourish. With that information in hand, the makers of copyright law might find a better balance between the interests of copyright industries and those of new creators and the public at large. That balancing point—cultural homeostasis—is where the edge of chaos and maximum sustainability will be found.

We are only now beginning to map the processes in the brain that produce human creativity and consider the environmental influences that encourage it. I have suggested that we should also map the workings of the copyright universe in order to identify, and use copyright law to encourage, an environment conducive to creativity. A systems approach, holistically analyzing the many complex adaptive systems interacting in the information ecosystem, offers a methodology for that task. The next chapter suggests some general guidelines and a few practical steps that would encourage lawmakers to approach copyright with a better understanding of the complex nature of copyright systems, assist researchers in gaining access to the necessary data to study copyright systems within a complexity framework, and assure that copyright laws ultimately respond to the results of such studies.

Chapter 5
Complexifying Copyright Law: A Possible Future for Copyright Lawmaking

If we want to craft copyright laws that encourage creativity, we must formulate legal rules that offer creators the opportunity to draw on elements of order and disorder as they seek to find the edge of chaos. The system of copyright law itself must balance on the same cusp if it is to be sustainable. This chapter considers the ways in which legislators and judges might draft and interpret copyright laws in ways that better recognize the complexity of the systems that produce creative expression. First, the chapter outlines some general lessons taken from complexity theory as a whole. The inherent nature of complex adaptive systems suggests some rules of thumb for legislative intervention in them. Systematic, empirical study of particular copyright systems should eventually offer more particular lessons that can be incorporated in legal treatment of specific copyright systems and subsystems. That work has not yet been done, so the chapter next suggests ways in which legislators can, if they will, facilitate the collection of useful data to enable empirical studies. Finally, the chapter suggests some legislative procedures that might ensure that copyright laws actually respond to the results of empirical inquiries. Judges, in their interpretation of those laws, could then look less to abstract theory and more to realities of copyright production as presented to them by the parties.

Rules of Thumb

General complexity rules for lawmakers can be summarized as: consider copyright systems holistically and in context; expect the unexpected; take the long view; leave room for creative chaos; nudge, don't shove; make simpler rules; be prepared to monitor the impact of interventions; and patiently make course corrections on a continuing basis.

Consider the Whole

Complexity theory teaches that the various elements of any complex adaptive system continuously coevolve with each other and with surrounding technological, social, political, and economic systems. Consequently, any legal tinkering with the rules of a system should take a comprehensive view of the system as a whole and the systems with which it interacts. Legislators taking a holistic approach will consider the impacts of new technologies and social structures on copyright industries, but must also bear in mind that that some creative destruction of preexisting business models may be economically desirable and that technological change may facilitate emergence of beneficial new social and political structures. It must consider the impacts of copyright-conserving technologies like digital rights management as well as copyright-challenging technologies like file sharing.

Expect the Unexpected

By its very nature, the system itself will continue to change before, during, and after attempts at legal intervention. Some emergent changes will be beneficial, others will not, since complex adaptive systems are morally neutral. Understanding of the nature of complex adaptive systems may help us formulate more effective legal responses to changes that emerge spontaneously in the copyright system. Of course, we also use legal intervention to actively instigate changes in the system, so understanding how such systems respond should guide our attempts to design effective laws. Any legal intervention is likely to produce unanticipated results. This does not mean that legal intervention is hopeless, but it does suggest that we adjust our expectations as to the likelihood and duration of successful regulation. Admitting that we cannot possibly foresee all the consequences of changes in copyright laws, we must attempt to regulate the systems within the limitations imposed by their natures and our own understanding, working as we do with brains that assume linear cause and effect relationships.

We are hampered by our own inability to comprehend the complexity of the systems we seek to regulate. Humans are not good at measuring the risks involved in situations that are too complicated to understand, as is the case with many of the complex technologies, from oil rigs to electronic networks, which we have created in the last century.[1] As popular as the phrase "butterfly effect" is, most people do not really grasp the fact that small changes may (or may not) cascade through complex systems and produce a range of effects. Consequently,

1 *See* David Brooks, *Drilling for Certainty*, N.Y. Times, May 27, 2010, at A23.

we gravitate toward simple, linear solutions to problems that are inherently complex and nonlinear. We assume that stronger copyright laws necessarily enhance copyright production, an assumption reflected in copyright's historical path towards copyright expansion. The whole utilitarian framework for copyright assumes a linear relationship between economic incentives and creativity that, as the preceding chapter illustrated, cannot possibly reflect the complexities of creative inspiration and production.

Take the Long View

Cause and effect relationships obviously do obtain over the short term in many situations, including copyright situations. Our brains also naturally focus more on the near, not the far, horizon. We must come to understand that, while the copyright system may be predictable over the short term, it will never remain so over the long term. Some factors are likely to remain the same as players in the copyright universe, like the scorpion and the frog, continue to behave according to their natures. Copyright owners will push legislators for stronger, more extensive copyright protections on the theory, whether supported by data or not, that more protection is always better. Industry lobbyists will influence legislators and administrators. Users will continue to share works not merely because it saves them money, but because human beings are inherently social creatures who build cultures. Creators will continue to create new works for this and more personal reasons. In the long term, however, the system as a whole will continuously respond to change in unpredictable ways that, in the current environment, will be particularly responsive to the ongoing revolution in electronic technologies. Legislators must learn to take the long view, seeking not only to protect past and present creators, but also to assure the availability of resources for the future creators of works whose contours we cannot presently imagine.

Allow Room for Creative Chaos

The long view requires recognition that the public domain is as important to creativity as copyright protection. The public domain stores and perpetuates the cumulative knowledge of humankind. It serves as the collective long-term memory from which all creators retrieve material for their creations. Copyright must remain permeable enough to allow works to flow into the public domain. It must also be sufficiently flexible to accommodate the chaos essential to creativity. The current attempt to ensure complete control to copyright owners through a combination of DRM and heavy-handed enforcement is neither consistent with copyright's history nor conducive to its role in enhancing creativity. While the manner in which we formulate copyright law seems unlikely to quash creativity entirely, it will certainly affect whether creativity is maximized or minimized.

Nudge—Don't Shove

The combination of the need for flexibility and the likelihood of unanticipated consequences indicate that gradually nudging the system toward the edge of chaos is preferable to the one-shot overhaul. Complexity economist Brian Arthur observed with respect to economic regulation:

> "[G]overnments should avoid both extremes of coercing a desired outcome or keeping strict hands off, and instead seek to push the system gently toward favored structures that can grow and emerge naturally. Not a heavy hand, not an invisible hand, but a nudging hand."[2]

Neither a completely free market nor the completely centralized economy will work in the long run. One is too chaotic, the other too rigid—neither is poised on the edge of chaos.

Given the nature of complex adaptive systems, copyright laws should be designed to encourage emergent, bottom-up solutions rather than imposing top-down solutions. The best-intentioned top-down solutions require inherently unreliable predictions about future system evolution and may cripple creative production rather than enhance it. While not all emergent behaviors will be desirable, they do represent responses to actual system conditions. If we sufficiently improve our information about the various components of the copyright system, we may be able to formulate copyright rules that gently nudge them, and the system as a whole, toward sustainability.

Simplify, Simplify, Simplify

As part of that process, lawmakers should consider the human agents in the system who will be directly impacted by new or altered rules. While lawmakers often seek overly linear solutions to complex problems, they also tend to embody those solutions in extremely complicated verbiage. Thus, we produce hellishly complicated statutes like the Copyright Act and the DMCA, many of whose provisions are incomprehensible to all but copyright specialists and sometimes

---

2 W. Brian Arthur, *Complexity and the Economy*, 284 Science 107–9 (April 2, 1999), *available at* http://www.santafe.edu/arthur/Papers/Papers.html.

obscure even to the judges tasked with interpretation of the provisions. Muddy rules like fair use and the idea/expression dichotomy are essential to reconcile copyright with First Amendment rights of expression. Yet they have become so complex in their construction and application that they offer little guidance to those affected by them. When copyright was exclusively the province of the copyright industries and their lawyers, such complication, while problematic, was manageable. Now that copyright directly impacts the daily lives of millions of ordinary people, simpler rules are advisable at least where individual users and creators of works are likely to be directly affected. If the owners of copyrighted content and satellite television and cable companies wish to draft absurdly complicated rules for broadcast of copyrighted content, let them deal with the consequences. Individual users who interact with copyrighted content on the Internet need simpler rules.

Complexity science teaches that complex behavior will arise even from simple rules, and simpler rules would certainly be easier for the average copyright consumer and creator to grasp. Perhaps lawmakers could develop clearly defined safe harbors for individual users—something like the guidelines created in the United States for educational fair use of copyrighted materials, though less detailed and less heavily tilted in favor of copyright owners. A number of scholars have pointed out that institution of the simple formality of cheap but recurring registration requirements for copyrights would free up an enormous number of orphan works for public use.[3] Such simple rules might have broad and beneficial effects.

The creation of simple rules may require lawmakers to abandon their traditional pattern of approving negotiated compromises drafted by major industry lobbyists. It also recommends against the creation of law by settlement of private disputes. The Google Book Settlement offers a perfect example of private negotiation, under judicial supervision, of an enormously complicated set of rules that, because of Google's dominance of Internet searches, could have come to govern the availability of vast amounts of copyrighted information. As a process, the settlement represented the antithesis of the holistic approach demanded by complexity theory; as a text, it exemplified the triumph of complication over simplicity. This kind of rulemaking is best left to legislators particularly since, once made, legal rules are difficult to undo.

---

[3] *See, e.g.*, Lawrence Lessig, *Copyright Policy: Orphan Works Reform*, LESSIG 2.0 (Feb. 1, 2007, 3:34 AM) http://www.lessig.org/blog/2007/02/copyright_policy_orphan_works.html.

Monitor the System

If we err in the copyright rules we make, path dependence and irreversibility of change in complex systems will prevent us from returning to our starting point. The path of law, like time, is unidirectional. Copyright laws once enacted tend to stay on the books, providing potential for later misuse. Witness the Semi-Conductor Chip Protection Act, passed in 1984 in a rush to protect chip manufacturers' mask works and essentially unused because it presumes a manufacturing method that chip makers quickly left behind. It is still in effect.[4] More problematically, the Audio Home Recording Act,[5] passed in 1992 to protect copyright owners from the anticipated revolution in digital audiotapes, provided a legal basis for attempts to kill the far more successful technology of the MPEG-1 or MPEG-2 Audio Layer III (MP3) player. At worst, ill-conceived copyright laws may actually create barriers to creative production by keeping the building blocks of knowledge out of the public domain. At best, where our interventions succeed in achieving our goals in the short term, our triumphs will be temporary because the system will continue to evolve. The arms race between content owners and technology users is as likely to continue as the race between predators and prey on the prairie.

All of which suggests that we should become accustomed to a more interactive relationship between copyright law and the copyright system. We must monitor the health of the system on a continuing basis and make regular adjustments to the legal rules to fine-tune its workings. As the copyright system is dynamic, so must copyright law be. The edge of chaos will always be a moving target. When legislative or judicial failures become manifest, we should redesign the laws in light of new realities and move forward. While we should certainly consider the empirical realities before laws are enacted, we should also engage in ongoing studies and regular reviews of the impact of copyright law on the system over time.

This is not currently the legislative pattern. Rather, drafters tend to operate in the belief that they can foresee all possible consequences of legislation and draft laws that will "accentuate the positive and eliminate the negative" impacts of the law on the system. They presume that legislative bodies can, in a single stroke, address the problem of, say, bootleg recordings of musical performances, or copyright protection of software, and never revisit the issue to determine whether the law actually works in practice. The 1976 revision of U.S. copyright law provides an

---

4 17 U.S.C. §§ 901–14 (2006).

5 17 U.S.C. §§ 1001–10 (2006).

example. The drafters worked on the codification for over 20 years, endeavoring to incorporate into the statute doctrines like fair use that courts had developed through centuries of litigation. Yet within a relatively short time span, the home computing revolution, digitization of content, and the commercialization of the Internet completely altered the information environment in ways that the revisers could not anticipate. Because of the inevitability of unanticipated change, the front end–loaded approach places a heavy burden on litigants and courts to handle the consequences of change on a case-by-case basis where the interests of the public and general policy concerns are not best represented.

While lawmakers should monitor the system continuously, they should not hasten to impose drastic new rules at the behest of threatened copyright industries without allowing a reasonable time for new emergent patterns to manifest themselves in the system. Courts, with their inherent conservatism, are sometimes better at exercising this sort of patience than legislators. Some judicial responses to technological change and copyright in recent decades are instructive. The U.S. Supreme Court's refusal to quash the videotape recorder industry at the behest of the movie studios proved enormously profitable for both industries as the videotape, and later digital versatile disk (DVD), markets for home viewing expanded. A carefully limited reading of the test for copyright infringement with respect to software permitted competition in the software market, providing consumers with more choice and software developers with market opportunities. Quite recently, the courts' refusal to shut down YouTube facilitated profitable ad-revenue-splitting agreements between YouTube's parent company, Google, and the copyright industries.[6] Legislative restraint in the drafting of copyright law, and judicial restraint in its interpretation, coupled with consistent monitoring of results, may encourage the development of similar opportunities in future.

Practical Steps

These general lessons from complexity theory have their uses, but they remain rather vague and theoretical. They leave open many questions as to the precise means by which to achieve a holistic, ongoing, interactive, relationship between copyright law and the copyright systems it governs. They resemble Learned Hand's "abstractions" analysis for drawing the line between ideas and expression in particular cases. He suggested in *Nichols v. Universal Pictures Corp.*, that

---

6 Claire Cain Miller, *YouTube Ads Turn Videos into Revenue*, N.Y.Times, Sept. 2, 2010, at B1.

> Upon any work, and especially upon a play, a great number of patterns of increasing generality will fit equally well, as more and more of the incident is left out. The last may perhaps be no more than the most general statement of what the play is about, … but there is a point in this series of abstractions where they are no longer protected, since otherwise the playwright could prevent the use of his "ideas," to which, apart from their expression, his property is never extended. … Nobody has ever been able to fix that boundary, and nobody ever can. [7]

This analysis may be a useful way of thinking about the problem of separating ideas from expression, but is something significantly less than a blueprint for actually deciding where to draw the line in a given case. So, too, the general rules of thumb just elucidated.

Legislators should develop a program for interactive management of the information ecosystem through copyright law. This book suggests that an essential step toward that goal is to build our understanding of the system itself through empirical investigation. Of late, the complete absence of factual support hardly seems to deter commentators in many fields from making entirely counterfactual claims. Nonetheless, resort to empirical fact remains the only objective route to governance of any system. Historically, one of the reasons for delegating copyright lawmaking to the industries has been that only the industries (and their lawyers, of course) really understood how their businesses worked and how copyright laws would impact them. One solution to industry domination of copyright lawmaking is to reduce the information imbalances among the industries, objective observers, legislators, and users. Empirical work by disinterested observers such as academics and nonprofit research institutes would make data about industry processes more widely available and allow legislators to make more objective determinations about how to craft the laws. The first task is, then, to develop means by which more data become available to researchers for analysis.

Accessibility of Data

Researchers themselves create and analyze survey data, subject to the usual difficulties of formulating appropriate questions and sampling representative populations. Some data are available directly from government entities. Historical data on copyright registrations in the US, for example, can be obtained from the Copyright Office, which publishes registrations annually and maintains records back to 1870. Historical archives, population records, and publicly available catalogs

---

[7] 45 F.2d 119, 121 (2d. Cir. 1930).

of creators and their works may all contain useful data. Most of these sources will not help, however, with the mapping of industry processes recommended herein. General information regarding the processes of some industries may be available, for example in the form of "how-to-break-into-the-industry" books, subject to the caveat that the processes change rapidly. Data regarding industry performance, much less tying process to performance, are likely to be more difficult to come by.

In the past, it was often difficult to acquire information such as sales data that might be shared in the industry, but not divulged to outside researchers. More such data is now available from the industries, though some of it may be too expensive for academic or nonprofit researchers. Subscriptions to industry databases can cost thousands of dollars. Oberholzer-Gee and Strumpf report, for example, that an academic subscription to Nielsen Soundscan, which reports sound recording sales, costs $10,000 per year; Nielsen's reports on video sales are even more expensive. Data on book sales are more reasonable, and some data on theatrical movie releases are available at no cost.[8] While research grants or research institutes might fund researchers in particular fields, some data will likely be beyond the financial reach of researchers. Additionally, some industries may keep crucial data closely held for strategic reasons. While voluntary cooperation between industries and independent researchers would certainly be the optimal way to build an overview of copyright systems, it may not be likely to occur without some assistance from lawmakers in the form of requiring data from proponents of copyright expansions.

Pre-enactment Analysis and Post-enactment Review

One such attempt was, in fact, made in the late 1980s. During the last years of his chairmanship of the key House of Representatives subcommittee that dealt with copyright, Congressman Robert Kastenmeier subjected proposed copyright legislation to a rough cost–benefits and policy analysis. Proponents of new protections were required to (1) show that the proposed interest fit harmoniously into the framework of existing law without violating its basic precepts; (2) articulate a reasonably clear definition of the new interest; (3) provide an honest analysis of all costs and benefits, and (4) establish that the enrichment of the public domain would outweigh the proprietary gains from enhanced protections.[9] This analysis

---

8 Felix Oberholzer-Gee and Koleman Strumpf, *File-Sharing and Copyright* 17 (2010), http://musicbusinessresearch.files.wordpress.com/2010/06/paper-felix-oberholzer-gee.pdf.

9 Robert W. Kastenmeier and Michael J. Remington, *The Semiconductor Chip Protection Act of 1984: a Swamp or Firm Ground*, 70 Minn. L. Rev. 417, 440–41 (1985).

was never more than a rule imposed through the personal power of the chairman and vanished, never to be revived, when Kastenmeier left the chairmanship in 1990, just as the controversies over the impact of digitization began to heat up.[10] The expansion of copyright accelerated rapidly in the late 1990s under the influence of copyright lobbyists. The Kastenmeier experiment constituted the first, and thus far only, attempt in the United States to require industries to supply empirical support for their requests for protection. The experiment was restricted to cost–benefit analysis, with policy overtones, and required an entirely front-end assessment, with no follow-up over time.

The European Union (EU) took a different approach to data collection when it enacted the Directive on Database Protection[11] that harmonized copyright treatment of databases and created a *sui generis* regime for databases not meeting the requirements for copyright protection. Rather than demanding that the industries produce data justifying protection in advance of legislation, the EU adopted the directive but required post-adoption assessment of whether the directive, after some years in operation, had achieved its goals. Using data from a survey of the EU database industry and the Gail Directory of Databases, which contains statistics on the growth of the database industry, the European Commission's Internal Market and Services Directorate General concluded that the directive had not, in fact, had the desired economic impact on database production in the EU and suggested several legislative options which were open for public comment.[12]

These experiences suggest that legislative bodies might more regularly require that data be provided by the industries seeking protection before legislative action and/or that data be collected and analyzed after enactment to test the impact of the law. That data could be used by legislatures or other government entities, but could also be made available publicly, at low or no cost, for use by independent researchers. For purposes of holistic systems analysis, the data should not be restricted to the kind of cost–benefit analysis demanded by the Kastenmeier

10 Lawrence Lessig, *The Balance of Robert Kastenmeier*, 2004 Wis. L. Rev. 1015, 1027–31 (2004).

11 Directive 96/9/EC of the European Parliament and of the Council of 11 March 1996 on the legal protection of databases, 1996 O.J. (L 77) 27.3, 20–28, *available at* http://eur-lex.europa.eu/smartapi/

cgi/sga_doc?smartapi!celexplus!prod!DocNumber&lg=en&type_doc=Directive&an_doc=1996&nu_doc=9.

12 *See* Commission of the European Communities, *DG Internal Market and Services Working Paper: First Evaluation of Directive 96/9/EC on the Legal Protection of Databases*, Dec. 12, 2005, *available at* http://ec.europa.eu/internal_market/copyright/docs/databases/evaluation_report_en.pdf.

standard. Cost–benefit analysis is, by its nature, linear and has limited predictive value. Moreover, any analysis coming from the industries is likely to be biased in their favor and must be checked by independent research. Legislatures should request mapping information about the industry, its inputs, outputs, and processes, as well as hard data about costs, sales, revenues, profits, and the like. While, clearly, industries should not be required to reveal valuable process information, such as trade secrets, a general overview of industry workings should do no harm and may already be compiled by industry sources or directories, or research performed by independent researchers.

The timing issue—collection before or after action—is a difficult one. If information is not already compiled at the time legislation is contemplated, it may be unlikely that it could be collected and analyzed before political pressures move the legislature toward action. The DMCA is representative—there was intense pressure to protect the content industries and no way to effectively predict the impact of such unprecedented legislation. On the other hand, some copyright legislation is under consideration for years before the legislature acts and, in those cases, consideration of empirical information before action is obviously desirable.

Certainly where pertinent information is available, Congress or any other legislative body should consider that information before adopting or expanding protective legislation. Even if the evidence does not derail the legislation, it may shape it by highlighting problem areas where limitations or exceptions are needed. The realities of lobbying influence and collective action problems probably ensure that even where such evidence is available, copyright expansions will occur. Consequently, after-the-fact monitoring may be even more essential than pre-enactment review of the realities on the ground. We might be wise to spend somewhat less time trying to predict all possible outcomes and somewhat more time finding out what actually did happen and adjusting the laws accordingly.

As in the case of the EU Database Directive, if industries seeking expanded protection claim that increased production will result from such protection, researchers can compare production data before and after enactment to determine whether, in fact, the legislation helped or hindered creative production. Copyright legislation, and paracopyright legislation like the DMCA or *sui generis* database protection laws, should require that baseline data be collected at the time of enactment and that, at a date certain after enactment, data again be compiled and an assessment made of the effectiveness of the law. The creation of a data repository and availability of the data to researchers should be a minimum requirement for an effective copyright regime. In this scenario, independent researchers may act as proxies for the public interest. The data should also be available to private parties involved in litigation, and through them, to judges sitting on copyright cases. Better-informed judges would, one hopes, produce better-balanced judgments.

In countries less politically allergic to centralized government than the United States, such a process might be lodged in new or existing agencies that exercise copyright oversight and those agencies might be charged with analyzing the data and reporting the results, as was the case with regard to the EU directive. In the United States, an attempt to create such oversight is likely to run headlong into vociferous objections against any government intrusion into markets (notwithstanding that copyright is, itself, an intrusion into markets) as well as budgetary restrictions.[13] One alternative might be to use existing agencies as collectors and repositories, but not analysts, of the data, which would be made available at low cost to independent researchers. In the United States, such duties accord with the Copyright Office's existing duties to maintain public records, provide guidance to Congress and the executive branch, and provide information services to the public, though not, perhaps, with its duties to promote copyright protection of U.S. works abroad.[14] Academics, research institutes, and other researchers could independently analyze the data and report their results through the usual venues of scholarly publications, press releases, and the like, opening issues to public debate. Or the Copyright Office might specifically contract out analysis to one or more independent research organizations tasked with reporting the results.

Follow Up

If the analyzed data show that creative production has increased as a result of the enactment, well and good—for the time being. But what if, as in the case of the database directive, the evidence indicates that the enactment has not resulted in more production or, worse, has had negative effects? Standing alone, such a system would provide no means for remedial legislative action beyond the current, flawed process. That process is unlikely to respond to the data by revising laws already on the books, leaving judges to interpret laws that are provably ineffective or even harmful. In the case of the Database Directive, the authors of the empirical

---

13 As a cautionary example, the Office of Technology Assessment provided Congress with independent advice on technological and scientific issues for over 20 years but was axed by the Republicans in 1995, a victim of conservative political and economic policies. The current climate is certainly no more favorable to such an enterprise.

14 U.S. Copyright Office, *A Brief Introduction and History*, Circular 1a, http://www.copyright.gov/circs/circ1a.html (last visited May 11, 2011).

study offered several alternatives: repeal of the directive, withdrawal of the *sui generis* part of the directive, amendment and clarification of the *sui generis* provisions, or maintaining the status quo.[15] Five years later, the status quo appears to have become the default position, and it seems likely that this will often be the case absent provision to the contrary. There are a couple of alternatives to this quandary: rolling reviews with consequences and sunset provisions. Somewhat surprisingly, the DMCA offers a template for a rolling review requirement.

During the debate over the DMCA, opponents raised serious concerns about the impact of this new form of protection on fair use rights. In response to those concerns, the drafters created a rolling review procedure requiring the Librarian of Congress to conduct rulemaking proceedings every three years. In those proceedings, the Librarian must examine claims that users will be inhibited by the act from their ability to make noninfringing uses of certain classes of copyrighted materials. The Librarian must consider several statutory criteria and must then publish any class of works for which she has determined that users will be adversely affected. Those works will be exempt from the circumvention provisions of the act for the succeeding three-year period.[16] To date most such exemptions have been exceedingly narrow, but there have been some surprises, such as the 2010 determination allowing users to circumvent Apple's encryption in order to use iPhone applications that are not Apple-approved.[17]

The DMCA procedure is limited in scope and only requires findings as to the availability of works, the impact on traditional fair uses, and the effect of circumvention on the copyright owner's market or the value of its works. It does empower the Librarian to respond directly to user claims. Some form of rolling review, if more widely applied in copyright law, and more explicitly requiring the collection of empirical data, could provide the necessary basis for continuous monitoring of the status of the copyright system. Any legislation expanding copyright or paracopyright protections might contain rolling review provisions requiring that, at relatively short intervals of three to five years, an empirical assessment of the impact of the legislation must occur. Such a time frame would allow researchers sufficient time to develop and present data without leaving the system unattended for too long. Similar requirements might be incorporated into

---

15 *DG Internal Market and Services Working Paper, supra* note 12, at 25–7.

16 17 U.S.C. § 1201(1)(C) (2006).

17 U.S. Copyright Office, *Rulemaking on Exemptions from Prohibition on Circumvention of Technological Measures that Control Access to Copyrighted Works*, http://www.copyright.gov/1201/ (last visited May 11, 2011).

trade agreements and treaties. Adoption of such a process would, however, raise questions as to where the power to respond to the findings should lodge.

In the United States, imposing the duty on the Librarian of Congress, or the Copyright Office, or the IP enforcement czar raises concerns about capture of the agency by industry lobbyists. The Copyright Office does not have a strong tradition of representing the interests of the public in copyright matters and has occasionally been criticized for favoring the industries, with whom it consults on a regular basis. The new IP czar is dedicated to enforcement against piracy, so balancing of owner interests against the public interest seems unlikely to come from that quarter. Similar concerns seem likely to arise in other countries with strong copyright lobbies. One option might be to create the position of national copyright ombudsman to represent the public's interest in the drafting process and in the process of assessment of the impact of legislation. Failing that, legislatures might specifically task the Register of Copyrights and similar officials, with assessing impacts on the public domain as well as on the industries. In certain narrowly defined areas, legislatures might confer on administrators the power to carve out exceptions and limitations in order to address concerns about the shrinking public domain. Such power, however, will not remove bad legislation from the books.

Add, then, another element: sunset provisions attached to each significant piece of copyright or paracopyright legislation. Such provisions might require, for example, that if assessment of impact data indicates that the law achieves its purpose or if the data are ambiguous, the law will continue in effect for the duration of another review period, at which time it will again be assessed. If the data show that the law clearly has no effect or a harmful effect, the law would lapse absent direct action by the legislature to mend it. Such provisions would not be appropriate for every small amendment to the copyright law, but would be desirable for major revisions or enactment of entirely new provisions like the DMCA in order to ensure that laws like AHRA do not linger on the books to cause litigation long after their initial purpose has disappeared.

An Illustration

The recommended process would require review of empirical data before copyright revision if possible, but would certainly provide for post-adoption empirical review and follow-up action based on the findings of that review. Recent proposals for extending copyright protection to fashion design can be used to illustrate how the process might work in a real context. Copyright protects fashion design in a number of countries, including France, but not in the United States.[18] The American fashion industry has sought copyright protection for fashion designs for years, as part of a long-running battle to extend copyright to design generally. Most recently, a bill that would extend copyright to fashion designs was introduced in the 112th Congress.[19] Unlike prior bills that failed to pass because their protections were deemed too broad, the new bill proposes a narrow approach that would protect only unique designs against substantially identical copies.[20]

Proponents of fashion protection argue that fashion designers lose sales because of knockoffs—claiming that hundreds of thousands of jobs are at risk because of fashion piracy. Arguments against enactment of such legislation rely on empirical knowledge about how the fashion industry works. In fashion, copying has benefits because of the cyclical nature of fashion trends—the so-called "piracy paradox." Fashion trendsetters wear expensive new designs; those designs are rapidly copied for cheaper knockoffs that then spread the new trend more widely to people who could never afford the originals—an entirely different market. The spread of knockoffs then pushes the trendsetters to seek out the next "new" thing and fashion designers must come up with new designs. Because of the peculiar nature of the industry, evidence indicates that copying actually accelerates creativity in fashion.[21]

Historical data also show that following the demise of the Fashion Originators' Guild, a fashion cartel struck down for antitrust violations, American fashion sales grew tremendously. Though some designers suffered losses during the recent recession, the apparel industry as a whole continued to grow. Apparel sales now exceed $300 billion per year and the industry employs millions of people. Fashion, moreover, is now available in cheaper forms to more and more consumers.[22] Offering copyright protection to fashion design might well destroy this lower-price market without offering additional incentive to high-end designers.

Under the proposed process, Congress should certainly consider available data before voting on any fashion protection bill. It should give thought to potential

---

[18] *See* Mary LaFrance, Global Issues in Copyright Law 17–24 (2009).

[19] The Innovative Design Protection and Piracy Prevention Act, HR. 2511, 112th Cong. (2011).

[20] Kal Raustiala and Chris Sprigman, *Why Imitation is the Sincerest Form of Fashion*, N.Y. Times, Aug. 12, 2010, at A23.

[21] Kal Raustiala and Chris Sprigman, *Should Fashion be Protected by Copyright Laws? A Guest Post,* N.Y.Times, Freakonomics (Mar. 12, 2010, 12:00 PM), http://www.freakonomics.com/2010/03/12/should-fashion-be-protected-by-copyright-laws-a-guest-post/.

[22] Raustiala and Sprigman, *supra* note 19.

impacts on the entire apparel industry, not just high fashion designers, and on both high- and low-end markets. It should, obviously, seek verification of the information about alleged job losses, industry cycles, revenues, and losses. Beyond that, a provision of the bill should require that, in the event Congress passes the bill, fashion design houses must provide verifiable base data about their current processes, revenues, losses, and so on, for purposes of later impact studies. The bill would provide for independent post-adoption review of the impact of enhanced protection on both high- and low-end markets at a date certain, say five years after passage, and should further provide what the consequences of that review should be.

The bill might provide, for example, that a review showing negative cumulative impact on the entire fashion industry would cause the bill to sunset. An entirely positive review might make the law permanent. A mixed review, showing, for example, enhanced sales for high fashion, but adverse impact on lower cost apparel providers or on availability to consumers, might trigger a series of rolling reviews over relatively short periods. A government agency, or independent research institute, might be charged with, or contracted with, for periodic monitoring of the impact of the bill to be followed by recommendations to Congress for alterations in the statute.

Advantages Going Forward

With data collection and availability as minimum requirements, legislatures could mix and match the length of review cycles, the agencies charged with review, the scope of authority conferred on those agencies, and the use of sunset provisions, as appropriate for different kinds of copyright legislation. Obviously, a process of preliminary fact finding coupled with after-the-fact review and legislative response would not cure problematic provisions already included in copyright law, but it might prevent future expansions where they are shown to be unnecessary. In the event of a major revision of copyright law, which seems unlikely to occur in the near future, such requirements might be applied more broadly to a larger range of statutory provisions. We would continue to rely on researchers and scholars to compile and analyze data regarding earlier changes in copyright law and their impact on creative production.

Over time, such an approach would encourage the development of a comprehensive overview of copyright systems and the impact of copyright law on them—a map of copyright's ecology supported by data describing and measuring its constituent parts and processes. Complexity models for copyright systems could capture key economic and noneconomic factors with better probabilistic predictive value. With these tools, the legislators drafting laws and the judges interpreting them might more carefully tailor copyright law to the actual requirements of real industries and to public interest concerns about the health of the public domain.

Starting from foundational rules that apply across copyright industries (if research supports the viability of such general rules), lawmakers would have both an empirical basis and a contextual framework to formulate different levels of protection for different kinds of works where differentiation seems warranted. Complexity studies would also help them respond in areas where copyright law has known deficiencies or faces entirely new circumstances. Immediate prospects include the treatment of collective, collaborative works (which copyright has never handled well), the newly burgeoning area of user-generated content, the problem of orphan works, and, increasingly, problems associated with the preservation, or lack thereof, of works captured in obsolete media or formats.

Summing Up

This chapter as a whole suggests that lawmakers seek to encourage bottom-up, emergent solutions with cautious, but regular, interventions through copyright law and that those interventions should be based, insofar as possible, on empirical fact. This is far from a libertarian agenda. The systems approach suggests that copyright law must be flexible enough to permit emergence because some emergent patterns will be highly beneficial. They will enhance creativity and the dissemination of information. However, some emergent patterns will be harmful, blocking creative uses or severely interfering with authors' remuneration. Unregulated economic systems produce emergent monopolies, financial crashes, and inequitable distributions of wealth. We regulate them, sometimes inadequately, to prevent abuses. We regulate our natural environment to control water uses, pollution, and the side effects of unconstrained development. Similarly, lawmakers must be prepared to control undesirable emergence in copyright law, including unanticipated effects of lawmaking itself. Only empirical studies can measure the effects, good and bad, of emergent patterns and legal intervention.

The complexity approach, relying on empirical study, does not fit in either of the high-protectionist or low-protectionist camps that dominate the current copyright debate. Empirically based mapping of copyright systems might well suggest a high-protectionist strategy for one system, but a low-protectionist strategy for another. The complexity approach seeks solutions that, in the context of real systems, will provide the stability and the flexibility necessary to enhance creative production and dissemination. Given the unpredictable nature of complex adaptive systems, lawmakers seeking copyright balance should nudge copyright systems toward middle ground, avoiding the all-property and no-property extremes. Legal rules should both provide stability and anticipate change, since change will inevitably occur and is manifestly occurring now in the copyright system. If it proves insensitive to developments in its surrounding environment, copyright law itself may ultimately fail, joining a lengthy list of inflexible complex systems consigned to the dustbin of history.

If the complexity approach must be aligned with any existing philosophy, it may fit into the rather loose collection of concepts known as Pragmatism, of which Holmes was the foremost proponent in law. Pragmatism emphasizes that various theoretical ideas may be useful but must be grounded in practical effects on real life.[23] Holmes favored a legal approach emphasizing the effect of experience, by which he meant the interaction of the human organism with its environment. John Dewey, another Pragmatist, insisted on situating the creative, artistic process firmly in the context of the real lives of both the artist and the audience, and in the interactive experience between the art object and its observer.[24] Pragmatism has enjoyed something of a resurgence lately, having been explicitly adopted by one Supreme Court Justice[25] and closely associated with incumbent President Barack Obama. Complexity theory certainly embraces the contextual and the process-oriented. It can, however, stand on its own as a theoretical framework to be tested against empirical reality, without the necessity of a philosophical flying buttress. It may align more closely with small-p pragmatism, in the sense of practical problem solving, than with any overarching philosophy.

By mapping the ecology of copyright, we can gradually build a copyright regime from the ground up, based not on abstract philosophies but on a growing body of information about copyright systems. If we develop a better understanding of what makes creative systems work, we may be able to craft a legal regime that actually does a better job of balancing the interests of past and future creators, disseminators, and users of expressive works. We could embark on a journey not unlike that commenced by evolutionary biologists after Darwin published *The Origin of Species*, in which the painstaking accumulation of data, and modification of theory to fit the data, reveal hitherto unsuspected interconnections,

---

23 Louis Menand, The Metaphysical Club 342–7 (2002).

24 John Dewey, Art as Experience 10–19 (1934).

25 Justice Breyer has recently embraced an essentially pragmatic approach to constitutional interpretation. *See* Stephen Breyer, Active Liberty: Interpreting our Democratic Constitution (2006).

dependencies, and capabilities of creative individuals and industries. It will take time to fill in the blanks on the ecosystem map. Over time, parts of the system will change like rivers shifting their courses, and the law must adjust accordingly. Our knowledge will never be perfect. Complexity theory recognizes such gaps but provides a methodology for identifying them and gradually filling them in, allowing lawmakers to craft better copyright laws, while recognizing that those laws will always be imperfect and will require long-term monitoring. Law will never be science, but it can, at least, be based in reality.

Some regions of copyright may prove resistant to complexity analysis and remain unmapped—"here be dragons." For those areas, other theoretical approaches may prove more fruitful. Nothing precludes resort to preexisting theoretical justifications where data are unavailable or complexity models appear to be inapposite. This book does suggest that philosophical justifications are of limited usefulness and must give way where they contradict the known facts. Nor does use of the complexity framework block off new theories or avenues of inquiry. Complexity theory is merely one more tool added to the toolbox with which we seek to improve our understanding of creativity, copyright systems, and the impact of law on creative production. If modern physics teaches us anything, it is that the complex universe, which we attempt to comprehend with our amazingly complex brains, seems to resist the imposition of a single unified theory of everything.

We have entered a new technological era in which we face the challenge, but also the opportunity, of adapting copyright law to the digital revolution. The decisions made in the next few years will affect the ecology of information for generations to come, for good or ill. The copyright rules we make will shape the copyright system we must live with. It is better, surely, to make those rules based on real information instead of on the unsubstantiated pleas of copyright owners or on philosophical positions established 300 years ago in a very different information ecosystem. Complexity theory offers a useful framework to undertake that task.

Bibliography

ADAMS, DOUGLAS. THE HITCHHIKER'S TRILOGY OMNIBUS EDITION (1983).

ALFORD, WILLIAM P. TO STEAL A BOOK IS AN ELEGANT OFFENSE (1995).

Alfred Bell & Co. v. Catalda Fine Arts, 191 F.2d 99 (2d Cir. 1951).

A & M Records, Inc. v. Napster, Inc. 239 F.3d 1004 (9th Cir. 2001).

ANDREASEN, NANCY C. THE CREATIVE BRAIN: THE SCIENCE OF GENIUS (2005).

Angier, Natalie. *Bringing New Understanding to the Director's Cut*, N.Y. TIMES, Mar. 1, 2010, at D1.

Arthur, W. Brian. *Competing Technologies, Increasing Returns, and Lock-In by Historical Events*, 99 ECON. J. 116–31 (March 1989), *available at* http://www.santafe.edu/arthur/Papers/Pdf_files/EJ.pdf.

Arthur, W. Brian. *Positive Feedbacks in the Economy*, 262 SCI. AM. 92–9, Feb. 1990.

Arthur, W. Brian. *Complexity and the Economy*, 284 SCIENCE 107–109 (April 2, 1999), *available at* http://www.santafe.edu/arthur/Papers/Papers.html.

Audio Home Recording Act, 17 U.S.C. §§ 1001–1010 (2006).

Authors Guild v. Google, Inc., 05 CIV.8136 (DC), 2011 WL 986049 (S.D.N.Y. Mar. 22, 2011).

BAK, PER. HOW NATURE WORKS: THE SCIENCE OF SELF-ORGANIZED CRITICALITY (1996).

Baker v. Selden, 101 U.S. 99 (1879).

Baker, Matthew J. and Brendan M. Cunningham, *Court Decisions and Equity Markets: Estimating the Value of Copyright Protection,* 49 J.L. & ECON. 567 (2006).

Baker, Matthew J. and Brendan M. Cunningham. *Law and Innovation in Copyright Industries*, 6(1) REV. ECON. RES. ON COPYRIGHT ISSUES 61–82 (2009), *available at* http://ssrn.com/abstract=1436160.

BBC News, *Rowling Seeks "Grotter" Ban*, Mar. 13, 2003, http://news.bbc.co.uk/2/hi/entertainment/2846105.stm.

BEINHOCKER, ERIC. D. THE ORIGIN OF WEALTH: EVOLUTION, COMPLEXITY, AND THE RADICAL REMAKING OF ECONOMICS 109 (2006).

Belluck, Pam. *To Tug at the Heart, Music First Must Tickle the Neurons*, N.Y. TIMES, Apr. 18, 2011, at D1.

BENKLER, YOCHAI. THE WEALTH OF NETWORKS: HOW SOCIAL PRODUCTION TRANSFORMS MARKETS AND FREEDOM (2006).

Bleistein v. Donaldson Lithographing Co., 188 U.S. 239 (1903).

Bobbs-Merrill Co. v. Straus, 210 U.S. 339 (1908).

Boden, Margaret A. The Creative Mind: Myths and Mechanisms (2d ed. 2004).

Boldrin, Michele and David K. Levine. Against Intellectual Monopoly (2008).

Boyle, James. *A Politics for Intellectual Property: Environmentalism for the Net*, 47 Duke L. J. 87 (1997).

Boyle, James. *The Second Enclosure Movement And The Construction Of The Public Domain,* 66 Law & Contemp. Probs. 33 (2003).

Boyle, James. The Public Domain: Enclosing the Commons of the Mind (2008).

Breyer, Stephen. *The Uneasy Case for Copyright: A Study of Copyright in Books, Photocopies, and Computer Programs*, 84 Harv. L. Rev. 281 (1970).

Breyer, Stephen. Active Liberty: Interpreting our Democratic Constitution (2006).

Brooks, David. *Drilling for Certainty*, N.Y. Times, May 27, 2010, at A23.

Buchanan, Mark. Nexus: Small Worlds and the Groundbreaking Theory of Networks (2002).

Bumiller, Elizabeth. *Battle Hymns around Campfires; ASCAP Asks Royalties from Girl Scouts, and Regrets it*, N.Y. Times, Dec. 17, 1996, at 1.

Buzsaki, Gyorgy. Rhythms of the Brain (2006).

Campbell v. Acuff-Rose Music, Inc., 510 U.S. 569 (1994).

Carr, Nicholas. The Shallows: What the Internet is Doing to our Brains (2010).

Carroll, Sean B. Endless Forms Most Beautiful (2005).

Cartoon Figures Run Afoul of Law, Chi. Trib., 27 Apr. 1989, at 26.

Casti, John L. Complexification: Explaining a Paradoxical World Through the Science of Surprise (1994).

Chamberlain v. Skylink, 381 F.3d 1178 (Fed. Cir. 2004).

Chander Anupam and Madhavi Sunder. *The Romance of the Public Domain*, 92 Cal. L. Rev. 1331 (2004).

Clark, Andy. *Out of Our Brains*, N.Y. Times, Opinionator (Dec. 12, 2010: 3:47 PM), http://opinionator.blogs.nytimes.com/2010/12/12/out-of-our-brains/.

Clark, Giles and Angus Phillips. Inside Book Publishing (4th ed., 2008).

Clifford, Ralph D. *Random Numbers, Chaos Theory, and Cogitation: A Search for the Minimal Creativity Standard in Copyright Law*, 82 Denv. U. L. Rev. 259 (2004).

Cohen, Patricia. *Charting Creativity: Signposts of a Hazy Territory*, N.Y. Times, May 8, 2010, at C1.

Cohen, Patricia. *Humanities 2.0: A New Enlightenment: Digital Keys to the Humanities' Riches*, N.Y. Times, Nov. 17, 2010, at C1.

Cohen, Patricia. *Analyzing Literature by Words, but Also by the Numbers*, N.Y. Times, Dec. 4, 2010, at C1.

Commission of the European Communities. *DG Internal Market and Services Working Paper: First Evaluation of Directive 96/9/EC on the Legal Protection of Databases*, Dec. 12, 2005, *available at* http://ec.europa.eu/internal_market/copyright/docs/databases/evaluation_report_en.pdf.

Computer Associates International, Inc v. Altai, Inc., 982 F.2d. 693 (2nd Cir. 1992).

Creative Commons. *Share, Remix, Reuse—Legally*, http://creativecommons.org/ (last visited May 9, 2011).

Dammann, Guy. *Harry Potter Breaks 400m in Sales*, The Guardian (Jun. 18, 2008), http://www.guardian.co.uk/business/2008/jun/18/harrypotter.artsandentertainment /.

Darnton, Robert. *A Digital Library Better than Google's*, N.Y. Times, Mar. 23, 2011, at A31.

Dawkins, Richard. The Selfish Gene (2d ed. 1989).

Dewey, John. Art as Experience (1934).

Dietrich, Arne. *Who's Afraid of a Cognitive Neuroscience of Creativity*, Methods 42 (2007) at 25.

Digital Millennium Copyright Act, 17 U.S.C. § 512, 1201–1205 (2006).

Directive 96/9/EC of the European Parliament and of the Council of 11 March 1996 on the Legal Protection of Databases, 1996 O.J. (L 77) 27.3, 20–28, *available at* http://eur-lex.europa.eu/smartapi/cgi/sga_doc?smartapi!celexplus!prod!DocNumber&lg=en&type_doc=Directive&an_doc=1996&nu_doc=9.

Doctorow, Cory. *Leaked Documents: UK Record Industry Wrote Web-Censorship Amendment*, Boing Boing (Mar. 11, 2010, 8:00 AM), http://boingboing.net/2010/03/11/leaked-documents-uk.html.

Doctorow, Cory. *HarperCollins to Libraries: We will Nuke your E-books after 26 Checkouts*, BoingBoing (Feb. 25, 2011, 12:41 PM), http://boingboing.net/2011/02/25/harpercollins-to-lib.html.

Donaldson v. Beckett, 1 Eng. Rep. 837 (H.L. 1774).

Dowling, John E. Creating Mind: How the Brain Works (1998).

Economics Focus: Agents of Change, The Economist, July 24, 2010, at 76.

Edwards, Harry T. *The Growing Disjunction between Legal Education and the Legal Profession*, 91 Mich. L. Rev. 34 (1992).

Electronic Frontier Foundation. *Anti-Counterfeiting Trade Agreement*, http://www.eff.org/issues/acta (last visited May 12, 2011.)

Farley, Joshua. Ecological Economics: Principles and Applications (2003).

Feist Publications, Inc. v. Rural Telephone Service Co., 499 U.S. 340 (1991).

FISHER, WILLIAM W. III. PROMISES TO KEEP (2004).

Folsom v. Marsh, 9 F.Cas. 342 (1841).

Genesis 1:28.

GLEICK, JAMES. CHAOS: MAKING A NEW SCIENCE (1987).

GNU Operating System. *What is GNU?*, http://www.gnu.org/ (last visited May 9, 2011).

Google Book Settlement, *Amended Settlement Agreement*, at http://www.googlebooksettlement.com/agreement.html (last visited May 11, 2011).

Gyles v. Wilcox, 26 ER 489 (1740).

Hardin, Garrett. *The Tragedy of the Commons*, 162 SCIENCE. 1243 (1968).

Harry Potter Brand Wizard, BLOOMBERG BUSINESS WEEK (July 21, 2005), http://www.businessweek.com/innovate/content/jul2005/di20050721_060250.htm.

HAWKINS, HARRIET. STRANGE ATTRACTORS: LITERATURE, CULTURE, AND CHAOS THEORY (1995).

Heller, Michael A. *The Tragedy of the Anticommons: Property in the Transition from Marx to Markets*, 111 HARV. L. REV. 621 (1998).

HESS, CHARLOTTE AND ELINOR OSTROM. UNDERSTANDING KNOWLEDGE AS A COMMONS: FROM THEORY TO PRACTICE 3–14 (2007).

Heverly, Robert. *The Information Semi-commons*, 18 BERKELEY TECH. L. J. 1127 (2003).

Hirsh, Aaron E. *Guest Column: Fish Shares and Sharing Fish*, N.Y. TIMES, THE WILD SIDE, Feb. 3, 2009 (10:00 PM), http://opinionator.blots.nytimes.com/2009/02/03/guest-column-fish-shares-and-sharing-fish/.

Hoffman, Jascha. *Killer Earth*, N.Y. TIMES MAGAZINE, Dec. 13, 2009, at MM49.

Hughes, Justin. *The Philosophy of Intellectual Property*, 77 GEO. L. J. 287 (1988).

INFORMATION INFRASTRUCTURE TASK FORCE. INTELLECTUAL PROPERTY AND THE NATIONAL INFORMATION INFRASTRUCTURE: THE REPORT OF THE WORKING GROUP ON INTELLECTUAL PROPERTY RIGHTS (1995).

Innovative Design Protection and Piracy Prevention Act, S. 3728, 111th Cong. (2010).

JERVIS, ROBERT. SYSTEM EFFECTS: COMPLEXITY IN POLITICAL AND SOCIAL LIFE (1997).

Jeweler's Circular Publishing Co. v. Keystone Publishing Co., 281 F. 83 (2d Cir. 1922).

JOHNSON, STEVEN. EMERGENCE: THE CONNECTED LIVES OF ANTS, BRAINS, CITIES, AND SOFTWARE (2001).

Judson, Olivia. *Where Tasty Morsels Fear to Tread*, N.Y. TIMES, OPINIONATOR (Sept. 29, 2009; 10:11 PM), http://opinionator.blogs.nytimes.com/2009/09/29/where-tasty-morsels-fear-to-tread/.

Kastenmeier, Robert W. and Michael J. Remington. *The Semiconductor Chip Protection Act of 1984:Aa Swamp or Firm Ground*, 70 MINN. L. REV. 417 (1985).

KAUFFMAN, STUART. AT HOME IN THE UNIVERSE: THE SEARCH FOR LAWS OF SELF-ORGANIZATION AND COMPLEXITY (1995).

Keim, Brandon. *Good Connection Really Does Lead to Mind Meld*, WIRED.COM, WIRED SCIENCE (Jul. 26, 2010, 3:00 PM), http://www.wired.com/wiredscience/2010/07/mind-meshing/.

Kelly, Kevin. *The New Socialism: Global Collectivist Society Is Coming Online*, WIRED, Vol. 17.06, May 22, 2009, *available at* http://www.wired.com/culture/culturereviews/magazine/17-06/nep_newsocialism.

Kirkpatrick, David D. *Publisher's Efforts to Keep Story's Secrets Collide with Free Speech*, N.Y. TIMES, June 21, 2003, at B6.

Kravets, David. *Special Interests See 'Classified' Copyright Treaty; You Can't*, WIRED (Oct. 14, 2009, 1:27 PM), http://www.wired.com/threatlevel/2009/10/specialinterests-peek-at-copyrighttreaty/.

Ku, Raymond Shih Ray. *The Creative Destruction Of Copyright: Napster And The New Economics Of Digital Technology,* 69 U. CHI. L. REV. 263 (2002).

Ku, Raymond Shih Ray, Jiayang Sun, and Yiying Fan. *Does Copyright Law Promote Creativity? An Empirical Analysis of Copyright's Bounty*, 62 VAND. L. REV. 1669 (2009).

LAFRANCE, MARY. GLOBAL ISSUES IN COPYRIGHT LAW (2009).

Lambert, Craig. *The Marketplace of Perceptions: Behavioral Economics Explains Why We Procrastinate, Buy, and Grab Chocolate on the Spur of the Moment*, HARVARD MAGAZINE, Mar.–Apr. 2006, at 50–57.

Landes, William M. and Richard A. Posner. *An Economic Analysis of Copyright Law*, 18 J. LEGAL STUDIES 325 (1989).

LANDES, WILLIAM M. AND RICHARD A. POSNER. THE ECONOMIC STRUCTURE OF INTELLECTUAL PROPERTY LAW (2003).

LARRABEE, AIMEE AND JOHN ALTMAN. LAST STAND OF THE TALLGRASS PRAIRIE (2001).

LAWLESS, ROBERT M., JENNIFER K. ROBBENNOLT, AND THOMAS S. ULEN. EMPIRICAL METHODS IN LAW (2010).

Lehrer, Jonah. *The Neuroscience of Inception*, WIRED.COM, WIRED SCIENCE, THE FRONTAL CORTEX (Jul. 26, 2010, 12:41 PM), http://www.wired.com/wiredscience/2010/07/the-neuroscience-of-inception/.

Leon v. Pacific Telephone & Telegraph Co., 91 F.2d 484 (9th Cir. 1937).

Lessig, Lawrence. *The Balance of Robert Kastenmeier*, 2004 WIS. L. REV. 1015 (2004).

Lessig, Lawrence. *Copyright Policy: Orphan Works Reform*, LESSIG 2.0 (Feb. 1, 2007, 3:34 AM) http://www.lessig.org/blog/2007/02/copyright_policy_orphan_works.html.

Lessig, Lawrence. *For the Love of Culture: Google, Copyright, and Our Future*. THE NEW REPUBLIC (Jan. 26, 2010, 12:00 AM), http://www.tnr.com/article/the-love-culture.

LEWIN, ROGER. COMPLEXITY: LIFE AT THE EDGE OF CHAOS (1992).

Lexmark v. Static Control Components, 387 F.3d 522 (6th cir. 2004).

Liebowitz, S.J. and Stephen Margolis. *Path Dependence, Lock-In, and History,* 11 J. L. ECON. & ORG. 205 (Apr. 1995), *available at* http://www.utdallas.edu/~liebowit/paths.html.

Liebowitz, Stan J. *Pitfalls in Measuring the Impact of File-Sharing on the Sound Recording Market*, 51 CESIFO ECON. STUD. 439 (2005), *available at* http://www.utdallas.edu/~liebowit/intprop/pitfalls.pdf.

LITMAN, JESSICA. DIGITAL COPYRIGHT (2001).

LOCKE, JOHN. TWO TREATISES OF GOVERNMENT, Book II, Ch. V ("Of Property") (c. 1690).

Love, James. *White House Shares the ACTA Internet Text with 42 Washington Insiders under Non Disclosure Agreements*, KNOWLEDGE ECOLOGY INTERNATIONAL (Oct. 13, 2009, 4:10 PM), http://kelonline.org/node/660.

Lunney, Glynn S. *Reexamining Copyright's Incentives-Access Paradigm,* 49 VAND. L. REV. 483, 606 (1996).

Madison, Michael J., Brett M. Frischmann, and Katherine J. Strandburg. *Constructing Commons in the Cultural Environment,* 95 CORNELL L. REV. 657 (2010).

Making Data Dance, THE ECONOMIST TECH. Q., Dec. 11, 2010, at 25, 26.

Markoff, John. *Striving to Map the Shape-Shifting Net*, N.Y. TIMES, Mar. 1, 2010, at D1.

Mazer v. Stein, 347 U.S. 201 (1954).

MENAND, LOUIS. THE METAPHYSICAL CLUB (2002).

MERRIAM WEBSTER'S COLLEGIATE DICTIONARY, 10th ed. (1997).

Metro-Goldwyn-Mayer Studios, Inc. v. Grokster, Ltd. 545 U.S. 913 (2005).

Millar v. Taylor, 98 Eng. Rep. 201 (1769).

Miller, Claire Cain. *YouTube Ads Turn Videos into Revenue*, N.Y. TIMES, Sept. 2, 2010, at B1.

Money Can Grow on Trees: Forests Are Disappearing Because They Are Undervalued, THE ECONOMIST, Sept. 25, 2010, at 6, 7, *available at* http://www.economist.com/node/17062651.

Mylly, Ulla-Maija. *Harmonizing Copyright Rules for Computer Program Interface Protection*, article draft, 2–3 (2009), copy in the author's possession.

Network Effects: How a New Communications Technology Disrupted America's Newspaper Industry—in 1845, The Economist, Dec. 19, 2009, at 142–4.

Nichols v. Universal Pictures Corp., 45 F.2d 119, 121 (2d. Cir. 1930).

Oberholzer-Gee, Felix and Koleman Strumpf. *The Effect of File Sharing on Record Sales: An Empirical Analysis* (2004), http://www.unc.edu/~cigar/papers/FileSharing_March2004.pdf.

Oberholzer-Gee, Felix and Koleman Strumpf. *File-Sharing and Copyright* 1 (2010), http://musicbusinessresearch.files.wordpress.com/2010/06/paper-felix-oberholzer-gee.pdf.

Olson, Mancur. The Logic of Collective Action: Public Goods and the Theory of Groups (1965).

Open Book. *Stinging the Dinosaurs*, Harvard Magazine, Nov.–.Dec 2008, at 26.

Orlowski, Andrew. *Apple, Tesco "Most to Blame" for Music Biz Crisis*, The Register (Oct. 19, 2007, 10:49 GMT), http://www.theregister.co.uk/2007/10/19/vrs_value_gap_report/.

Ostrom, Elinor. Governing the Commons: The Evolution of Institutions for Collective Action (1990).

Patterson, L. Ray and Stanley W. Lindberg. The Nature of Copyright: A Law of Users' Rights (1991).

Patterson, L. Ray and Stanley F. Birch, Jr. *A Unified Theory of Copyright* (Craig Joyce ed., 2009), 46 Hous. L. Rev. 215 (2009).

Perfect 10, Inc. v. Amazon.com, Inc., 508 F.3d 1146 (9th Cir. 2007).

Pierson v. Post, 3 Cai. R. 175, 2 Am. Dec. 264 (N.Y. Sup. Ct. 1805).

Png, Ivan P.L. and Qiu-Hong Wang. *Copyright Duration and the Supply of Creative Work* (Sept. 2006), http://papers.ssrn.com/sol3/papers.cfm?abstract_id=932161.

Raichle, Marcus E. *The Brain's Dark Energy,* Sci. Am., Mar. 2010, 44–9.

Rampell, Catherine. *They Did Their Homework (800 Years of It),* N.Y. Times, July 2, 2010, at BU1.

Raustiala, Kal and Chris Sprigman. *Should Fashion be Protected by Copyright Laws? A Guest Post,* N.Y. Times, Freakonomics (Mar. 12, 2010, 12:00 PM), http://www.freakonomics.com/2010/03/12/should-fashion-be-protected-by-copyright-laws-a-guest-post/.

Raustiala, Kal and Chris Sprigman. *Why Imitation is the Sincerest Form of Fashion*, N.Y. Times, Aug. 12, 2010, at A23.

Rose, Carol M. *The Comedy of the Commons: Custom, Commerce, and Inherently Public Property*, 53 U. Chi. L. Rev. 711, 723 (1986).

Rose, Carol M. *The Several Futures of Property: Of Cyberspace and Folk Tales, Emission Trades and Ecosystems*, 83 MINN. L. REV. 129 (1998).

Rose, Carol M. *Romans, Roads, And Romantic Creators: Traditions Of Public Property in the Information Age*, 66 LAW & CONTEMP. PROBS. 89 (2003).

ROWLING, J.K. HARRY POTTER AND THE PHILOSOPHER'S STONE (1997).

Rowling, J.K. J.K. ROWLING OFFICIAL SITE, http://www.jkrowling.com/en/ (last visited May 9, 2011).

Ruhl, J.B. *Complexity Theory as a Paradigm for the Dynamical Law-And-Society System: A Wake-Up Call for Legal Reductionism and the Modern Administrative State*, 45 DUKE L. J. 849 (1996).

Ruhl, J.B. and Harold J. Ruhl, Jr., *The Arrow of the Law in Modern Administrative States: Using Complexity Theory to Reveal the Diminishing Returns and Increasing Risks the Burgeoning of Law Poses to Society*, 30 U.C. DAVIS L. REV. 405 (1997).

Ruhl, J.B. *Law's Complexity: A Primer*, 24 GA. ST. U. L. REV. 885 (2008).

Samuelson, Pamela. *Enriching Discourse on Public Domains*, 55 DUKE L. J. 783, 786–813 (2006).

Sandoval, Greg. *U.K Embraces "Three Strikes" for Illegal File Sharing*, CNETNEWS, Apr. 8, 2010, http://news.cnet.com/8301-31001_3-20002018-261.html.

SAWYER, KEITH. EXPLAINING CREATIVITY: THE SCIENCE OF HUMAN INNOVATION (2006).

Scholastic, Inc. v. Stouffer, 221 F. Supp. 2d 425 (S.D.N.Y. 2002).

Sega Enterprises, Ltd. v. Accolade, Inc., 977 F.2d 1510 (9th Cir. 1992).

Semi-Conductor Chip Protection Act, 17 U.S.C. §§ 901–14 (2006).

Shadbolt, Nigel and Tim Berners-Lee. *Web Science Emerges*, SCI. AM. (Oct. 2008), at 76–81.

Shermer, Michael. *Captain Hook Meets Adam Smith*, SCI. AM., Oct. 2009, at 34.

Shiller, Robert J. *An Echo Chamber of Boom and Bust*, N.Y. TIMES, August 29, 2009, at BU5.

SHIRKY, CLAY. COGNITIVE SURPLUS: CREATIVITY AND GENEROSITY IN A CONNECTED AGE (2010).

Silbey, Jessica. *Harvesting Intellectual Property*, *Abstract*, http://ssrn.com/abstract=1599747.

Sony Corp. of America v. Universal City Studios, Inc. 464 U.S. 417 (1984).

Statute of Anne, 1710, 8 Ann., c.19 (Eng.).

STEIN, KATHLEEN. THE GENIUS ENGINE: WHERE MEMORY, REASON, PASSION, VIOLENCE, AND CREATIVITY INTERSECT IN THE HUMAN BRAIN (2007).

STRAUCH, BARBARA. THE SECRET LIFE OF THE GROWN-UP BRAIN: THE SURPRISING TALENTS OF THE MIDDLE-AGED MIND (2010).

SULLIVAN, WILLIAM M., ANNE COLBY, JUDITH WELCH WAGNER, LLOYD BOND, AND LEE S. SHULMAN. EDUCATING LAWYERS: PREPARATION FOR THE PROFESSION OF LAW (2007).

Thadeusz, Frank. *No Copyright Law: The Real Reason for Germany's Industrial Expansion?*, SPIEGEL ONLINE (Aug. 18, 2010, 4:52 PM), http://www.spiegel.de/international/zeitgeist/0,1518,druck-710976,00.html.

Turner, Michael S. *Origin of the Universe*, SCI. AM., Sept. 2009, at 36.

U.S. CONST., Art. I, § 8, cl. 8.

U.S. Copyright Act, 17 U.S.C. §§ 102, 107, 109, 115, 302–304.

U.S. Copyright Office. *A Brief Introduction and History*, Circular 1a, http://www.copyright.gov/circs/circ1a.html (last visited May 11, 2011).

U.S. Copyright Office. *Rulemaking on Exemptions from Prohibition on Circumvention of Technological Measures that Control Access to Copyrighted Works*, http://www.copyright.gov/1201/ (last visited May 11, 2011).

Venkataraman, Bina. *Finding Order in the Apparent Chaos of Currents*, N.Y. TIMES, Sept. 29, 2009, at D1.

WALDROP, M. MITCHELL. COMPLEXITY: THE EMERGING SCIENCE AT THE EDGE OF ORDER AND CHAOS (1992).

Walsh, Bryan. *Sustainable Sushi,* TIME, Oct. 27, 2008, at 56.

WALTER, MICHEL M. AND SILKE VON LEWINSKI. EUROPEAN COPYRIGHT LAW: A COMMENTARY (2010).

Warner Bros Ent., Inc. v. RDR Books, 575 F.Supp.2d 513 (S.D.N.Y. 2008).

Watson, Julie and Tomas Keliner. *J.K. Rowling and the Billion-Dollar Empire*, FORBES.COM (Feb. 26, 2004), http://www.forbes.com/2004/02/26/cx_jw_0226rowlingbill04.html.

WIPO Copyright Treaty, Dec. 20, 1996, *available at* http://www.wipo.int/treaties/en/ip/wct/trtdocs_wo033.html#P87_12240.

WIPO.INT. *Berne Convention for the Protection of Literary and Artistic Works*, Sept. 9, 1886 as revised and amended through Sept. 28, 1979, *available at* http://www.wipo.int/treaties/en/ip/berne/rtdocs_wo001.html (last visited May 9, 2011).

WIPO Performances And Phonograms Treaty, Dec. 20, 1996, *available at* http://www.wipo.int/treaties/en/ip/wppt/trtdocs_wo034.html.

WTO.ORG. *TRIPs: Text of the Agreement*, Apr. 15, 1994, *available at* http://www.wto.org/english/tratop_e/trips_e/t_agm0_e.htm (last visited May 9, 2011).

Yu, Peter K. *Intellectual Property and the Information Ecosystem*, 2005 MICH. ST. L. REV. 1 (2005).

Index